M

MUSIC AS YOGA

MUSIC AS YOGA

Sri Swami Sivananda

Published by

THE DIVINE LIFE SOCIETY
P.O. SHIVANANDANAGAR—249 192
Distt. Tehri-Garhwal, Uttaranchal, Himalayas
INDIA

Price]   2007   Rs. [50/-

First Edition: 1956
Second Edition: 2007
[1,000 Copies]

ES 21

· Published by Swami Vimalananda for
The Divine Life Society, Shivanandanagar, and printed by
him at the Yoga-Vedanta Forest Academy Press,
P.O. Shivanandanagar, Distt. Tehri-Garhwal, Uttaranchal,
Himalayas, India

SRI SWAMI SIVANANDA

Born on the 8th September, 1887, in the illustrious family of Sage Appayya Dikshitar and several other renowned saints and savants, Sri Swami Sivananda had a natural flair for a life devoted to the study and practice of Vedanta. Added to this was an inborn eagerness to serve all and an innate feeling of unity with all mankind.

His passion for service drew him to the medical career; and soon he gravitated to where he thought that his service was most needed. Malaya claimed him. He had earlier been editing a health journal and wrote extensively on health problems. He discovered that people needed right knowledge most of all; dissemination of that knowledge he espoused as his own mission.

It was divine dispensation and the blessing of God upon mankind that the doctor of body and mind renounced his career and took to a life of renunciation to qualify for ministering to the soul of man. He settled down at Rishikesh in 1924, practised intense austerities and shone as a great Yogi, saint, sage and Jivanmukta.

In 1932 Swami Sivananda started the Sivanandashram. In 1936 was born The Divine Life Society. In 1948 the Yoga-Vedanta Forest Academy was organised. Dissemination of spiritual knowledge and training of people in Yoga and Vedanta were their aim and object. In 1950 Swamiji undertook a lightning tour of India and Ceylon. In 1953 Swamiji convened a 'World Parliament of Religions'. Swamiji is the author of over 300 volumes and has disciples all over the world, belonging to all nationalities, religions and creeds. To read Swamiji's works is to drink at the Fountain of Wisdom Supreme. On 14th July, 1963 Swamiji entered Mahasamadhi.

PREFACE

Music is the subtlest of the Fine Arts. Painting, Sculpture, Literature and all other avenues of human emotional expression have the advantage of form of some kind, of being able to appeal to the human mind through the eye, a more satisfactory sense than the ear, and of comparative stability of existence or duration. The forms can be seen, kept steady for constant inspection and even corrected over and over again, if need be. But Music has no facility of this sort. Originating as invisible sound, lingering in the air for but the barest fraction of a moment, it disappears into ether, leaving not a tangible trace behind for verification even, let alone correction. In its effects and influence on the human mind, however, it is more universal than others: even the grossest forms of the other arts can be neither enjoyed nor appreciated by any one who has not had some preparation or training in these respective arts and their functioning principles. But Music is for all: from inanimate objects to consciousness-transfigured Yogi, every bit of creation is subject to its sway to a smaller or greater extent; and if there is any agency under the sun which can make Man, with all his conflict of feelings and passions and with, sorrow, disease and death dogging him at every step, forget all of them for at least a blissful moment of unalloyed pleasure, it is music and music alone. That this form of art happens to be also a delectable medium for getting into tune with the Infinite is one of the favours bestowed on Mankind by a merciful providence.

This wonderful art had been widely cultivated in India and had attained a high level of perfection at least 3,000 years ago. It was in fact one of the unmistakable indications to us of the high state of civilisation which the people of the land had reached even in those early times. What distinguished Indian Music, however, from its prototypes in other climes was its outlook and tendency: it was never regarded in India as a mere lay art, as a mere system of pleasing the sensuous part of man. It was always held to be but an extension and outward symbolisation of the Omnipresent Pranava Sound—OM—and utilised only for purposes of God attainment—a feature it has retained to the present-day, as will be evident from the fact that, up to the end of the last century, the subject of musical compositions has rarely been anything but God and His glories.

The system of music developed along these lines was originally one and the same throughout the vast land and had a supreme unity of nature and purpose. From the early eras of the Christian century, however, the northern part of the peninsula came to be coloured by the impact of Arabic, Persian and Moghul civilisations. As a result, it began to show increasingly certain natural and inevitable modifications in practice and came gradually, in course of time, to be labelled the northern or Hindustani Music. The South, which was protected from such onsets by its geographical position, escaped from coming under the sway of these influences; and the original system accordingly was preserved there in a purer condition and is flourishing even today under the appelation, Carnatic Music. But it is well known that both these systems are of the same origin and substance, though, of course, considerable variations have manifested themselves owing to growing differences in the styles of expression.

Just like all other forms of art, Indian Music also was for a long time confined to its practical and operative aspect. As soon, however, as practice had developed sufficient growth and variety, theoretical expositions of the subject began to appear. These were, of course, something in the nature of a necessity, if the practical secrets of the art, garnered by centuries of experience, were to be preserved from oblivion and corruption.

These treatises on Music were accordingly a record of the practices up to their respective dates and functioned naturally as a grammar of rules on that basis for subsequent guidance. Narada, Bharata, Saranga Deva, Purandara Dasa, Venkatamahi and a host of others form a glorious galaxy of musician-grammarians who earned immortal names for themselves by leaving to posterity rich treasure troves of musical knowledge. In the treatises left by them we have clear and accurate expositions of the principles governing musical practice—the differentia and genius of the various Ragas and Melas, the nature and operation of the distinctive Gamakas and other important points calculated to give a practitioner a firm and comprehensive grasp of his chosen field. These therefore, served both as a record of the achievements up to their time in the theory and practice of Indian Music as well as a stimulant to further research and progress.

It is not to be expected, however, that such treatises, though numerous, exercised by themselves any practical influence on, or were even available to, all and sundry in the music world. Only a few fortunate and gifted individuals had access to them and used them as guide for themselves and the basis of further developments; the rank and file of the votaries of the art were content to carry on the traditional system of learning only by the ear, without any reference to the existent grammars, and to hand torch on to their successors in similar fashion. After all; the growth of any form of art is never appreciably dependent on the rules and grammars on the subject but is more the result of uninterrupted and rich tradition in the practice of the art. The art of music is no exception to the rule. Speaking generally, we find that what kept Carnatic Music on such a high level of excellence are not the grammatical rules and regulations laid down from time to time but the careful preservation and fostering of the rich heritage of practice by

[8]

generation after generation through the Gurukula system of musical education.

There is no need to dilate on this, as everyone in India is familiar with the phenomenon directly or by hearsay. But a special factor that worked in the same direction and contributed to the same result deserves mention here. It is a fact admitted on all hands that the special feature and glory of Carnatic Music is its Raga system and that for rendering a Raga with verve and truth of expression wide "hearing" constant practice, considerable experience, rich imagination and flair for artistic effects are the *sine qua non*. This is only to say that the Raga is the keystone of musical architectonics and that on the preservation of its purity depends the well-being of the whole melodic system. The invention of a device for mapping out the all-important Raga and the handling of the device with brilliant efficiency is the special factor adverted to above. The reference, of course, is to the musical form of composition known as the Kirtan or Kriti. It is impossible to imagine a more suitable or satisfactory method for fixing the contour and trends of a Raga and making a blueprint of it, so to say, leaving at the same time plenty of scope for imaginative handling of the same. What better medium can be conceived of for preserving the outlines of the special ambulation of each particular Raga than a composite picture of it, which the Kriti is? Even today, you will find eminent professors engaged in the ticklish task of laying down the grammar of Raga sedulously investigating all the Kritis in that Raga as sung by various authoritative exponents in the past and clinching the issues only after such exhaustive comparisons. It must also be a matter of common experience that beginners in music who want to distinguish and recognise Ragas like Ananda Bhairavi, Yadukula Kamboji, Nilambari, etc., are always advised by knowledgeable persons to take one or two Kritis in those Ragas as infallible patterns to guide them to the spirit of the Ragas. This, again, is also why great pioneers

[9]

who design a new Raga (for the first time) invariably take the precaution of composing one or more Kirtans in that Raga, laying thereby down, as it were, the four corners of the new Raga for the guidance of others

This Kriti form of composition, so reliable an indicator of Raga tendencies and the sheet anchor of Carnatic music, has been handled by numberless composers from the time of its invention by Thalappakkam Chinnayya in the 15th Century A.D. Many of them have been outstanding geniuses and left behind them a rich legacy of soul-stirring Kirtans. But it is sad to have to record also that the greater portion of this has been allowed to be lost. Lacking the means of permanent recording and easy duplication, few of them used to keep any systematic records or copies of their composition pieces. A few notes jotted down now and then by a composer, excerpts made from the originals by admiring pupils—these form the extent of the records that have come down to us! The result was that, when a particular singer who had sole custody of some Kirtans shuffled off his mortal coil, those Kirtans promptly joined him where he was. They were lost to posterity once for all! The magnitude of the loss sustained in this way and by accidents is simply staggering. A few instances will serve to give one an idea: Tradition has it that Purandara Das, entitled to be called, so far as an individual can be so called, the Founder of Carnatic Music because of his abundant and meritorious services to it, composed as many as 5,00,000 Kritis; today the most diligent search would probably fail to unearth more than 500! Kshetragna, it is believed, left over 4,000 of his inimitable Padas we can call ourselves lucky if we can lay our hands on even 200 (and even these are on the eve of permanent disappearance)! There is evidence to show that Thyagaraja, who lived barely a hundred years ago, composed no less than 24,000 Kritis (it will be noticed with interest that the number is the same as the total number of verses in Valmiki Ramayana);

[10]

700-800 is the utmost we could boast of being able to recover! It is the sacred duty of all Nada Yogis to preserve the Kritis that the unique good fortune of the present generation and the Lord's Supreme Grace has preserved so far; and further enrich music by adding soul-elevating compositions in praise of the Lord and vividly portraying the evanescent nature of the tantalising pleasures of this world and the eternal nature of the Bliss of communion with the Lord. Thus would they render a double-service: spiritually elevating the people and preserving the grandeur of our music.

May God bless all the Nada Yogis of the world! May you all attain God-realisation in this very birth, by singing the Lord's Names and glories!

Sivananda

REALISATION THROUGH MUSIC

**(Swamiji's speech on the 109th Anniversary Day
of Saint Thyagaraja)**

Sri Thyagaraja Swami is called Nada Brahma Swami. He is the greatest songster-saint which the world has ever produced.

He was born in South India in Tanjore District, of a poor Brahmin family. He had direct Darshan of Lord Rama. A great music festival is conducted every year in Tiruvayur six or seven miles from Tanjore, on the banks of Cauvery. All the greatest musicians of India go there and pay their homage to this great saint.

Several thousands of songs he has sung,—all spontaneous outpourings from the heart. They were not the result of exertion or effort. Once a Raja asked him to praise him and offered to give him a great donation including pearls. He totally refused. He said, "My tongue cannot praise human beings. It can praise only Lord Rama." It is said that Lord Rama Himself carried his palanquin and brought water for his ablution. Such was the greatness of the saint Thyagaraja. He was full of love and devotion to the Lord and he had direct Darshan of the Lord and had also Cosmic Consciousness.

We too can attain Lord's Darshan through singing Kirtan and songs. There are various ways to God-realisation, Bhakti Yoga, Raja Yoga, and other Yogas. But the easiest, cheapest, quickest, safest and surest way to attain God-realisation is Sankirtan Yoga. Just as a deer is entrapped by music, so also the mind which is also as restless and wandering as the deer, is steadied by the music and made to dissolve in Brahman. By the singing of Kirtans and songs in praise of the Lord, the mind

[12]

melts and becomes one with the Lord. Therefore, let us also pray to the Lord, sing His Kirtans and attain God-realisation this very second.

God-realisation is not difficult. It is easy for those who are engaged in uttering His Name and singing His praise and meditating on His feet, and who have surrendered themselves to the Lord.

So we request the Thyagaraja devotees, Swami Amarananda, Swami Sadasivananda, Swami Nada Brahmananda, and Swami Santananda to give their outpourings. Om.

The path of devotion is the easiest and the surest of all the ways for attaining emancipation. The science of music goes hand in hand with Bhakti Yoga.

Sangeeta is the fountain-source of all our being. It has an emotional appeal to the inner aspiration of humanity.

Even inanimate objects are moved by the music. There is music of the planets. All arts aspire towards the condition of music. Through music the soul learns harmony and rhythm and an even disposition to justice. Rhythm and harmony find their way into the secret notches of the soul and keep it entirely oblivious of the outside world, in sublime peace.

A devotee sings Bhajan and forgets everything and submerges himself in Srutilaya.

When a sincere devotee sings there is the harmonious blending of Rasa, Bhava, and Rachana in his songs, as form, colour and fragrance in the rose.

Nritya that accompanies a Kirtan is an inseparable, sacred movement of the various limbs of the body in accordance with the inner divine Bhav. Nritya is a divine science. Those who do Nritya should bring out the six Bhavas: Shrishti, Samhar, Vidya, Avidya, Gati and Agati. It is an external manifestation induced in Bhaktas by the thrill of ecstasy from within and helps

[13]

the devotees in merging themselves in the Lord. Supreme joy and magnanimity of this sacred Nritya should only be understood by Rishis and devotees like Narada, Vyasa, Sukadev, Mira, Tukaram, Gouranga, Hafiz and others and not by the worldly-minded persons whose minds are saturated with passion. The Adi Gurus for this celestial Nritya were Lord Siva, Krishna and Mother Kali. Dancing that accompanies vulgar music and obscene songs with intoxicants is invariably the outcome of passion and base thoughts. It has a deep tinge of lust. Do you see clearly the difference now friends?

MUSIC AS YOGA

MUSIC AS YOGA

MUSIC: A YOGA SYNTHESIS

Only Thyagaraja could worship Nadabrahman. You must be the very greatest among the renunciates if you are to adore the Lord through the direct adoration of His Supreme Name, His First Manifestation, viz., Nada or Pranava. Not a parrot-like repetition of the words, not a masterly rendering of the music, perfectly set to Raga and Tala; but singing with the heart, playing on the inner Veena on the strings of Bhakti and Prema, alone will enable you to enter into the spirit of Thyagaraja.

Music attracts every living being. Music melts the hardest heart. Music softens the brutal nature of man. Music heals man of a million maladies. Wherefrom has music derived this mighty power? From the Supreme Music of Brahman, the Sacred Pranava. Listen to the vibration of the Tambura or the Veena: do you hear the majestic Pranava-Nada? All the musical notes are blended beautifully into this Pranava. All the musical notes spring from this Pranava. Music is intended to reverberate this Pranava-Nada in your heart. For OM or the Pranava is your real name, your real Swarupa. Therefore, you love to hear music which is but the most melodious intonation of your own essential name. When the mind thus gets attracted and unified with one's essential nature, the great Power of God stored up there wells up within and heals body and mind. The Bhakta enters into Bhava-Samadhi by singing devotional music. He comes face to face with the greatest storehouse of Knowledge and Wisdom, Ananda or Supreme Bliss. Therefore, he emerges from this Samadhi as a Jnani and radiates Peace, Bliss and Wisdom all round.

Such a Para-Bhakta or Jnani was Thyagaraja. Such is this glorious Music Yoga which Thyagaraja gave to the world. It was because Thyagaraja could enter into the very soul of each

Raga that he could compose songs that would be in conformity with the Raga-Bhava. This harmony between the Raga-Bhava and the Bhava of the Kriti that evokes in the heart of the person singing that Kriti, the Bhava that Thyagaraja filled it with. There is mighty spiritual force, spiritual power in the Kritis. Therefore, they have been immortalised. As long as man utters sounds, so long will Thyagaraja Kritis remain; and so long will the undying fame of this Supreme Sovereign of the Music World, the Prince among Music Yogins, endure and inspire thousands and thousands of Sadhakas to take this path of sweet Music Yoga and attain union with the Paramatma, whose first manifestation was the Music of the Pranava.

Music is a synthesis of the various Yogas or paths to God-realisation. Besides, it enjoys the unique privilege of defying one of fundamental spiritual doctrines, viz., that which is pleasant is not good, and that which is good is not necessarily pleasant. It is in music that you find the sole exception to this rule. It is both pleasant and good—Preya and Sreya, in the terminology of the Kathopanishad.

Music, like Krishna Lilas, caters to people of all temperaments, wins the hearts of all and transforms all beings—human, sub-human and superhuman. Devas, even the Trinity (Brahma, Vishnu and Siva) are pleased and easily propitiated by music. What to say of human beings, even animals are charmed and tamed by sweet, melodious music.

Music itself is Hatha Yoga Sadhana: for it involves a good amount of control and regulation of breath. There is deep and full breathing; and this greatly strengthens the lungs and purifies the blood, too.

Moreover, the various musical notes have their own corresponding Nadis (subtle channels in the vital sheath of the body) in the vital centres within—the Kundalini Chakras—and music vibrates these Nadis, purifies them and awakens the psychic and spiritual power dormant in them. Purification of Nadis, not only ensures peace and happiness of mind, but goes a long way in Yoga Sadhana and helps the aspirant to reach the goal of life very easily.

Trapped in music, the mysterious mind with its thousand hoods of Vasanas and Vrittis, lies quiescently on the lap of the Sadhaka; and he can make it dance to his tune, control it according to his will and mould it as he pleases. Mind, the instrument of Satan in man, the magic wand of Maya, the terror of all spiritual aspirants, is there in the hands of this Music Yogi under his perfect control. The wonder of wonders in the case of this Music Yoga is that it is not only the musician whose mind is thus controlled, but the minds of all those who listen to music become calm, peaceful and blissful. That is why great Saints like Mira Bai, Tukaram, Kabir Das, Sri Thyagaraja, Purandaradasa and others wove their Upadesha into sweet music: with the sweet music, these sublime thoughts would easily get into the heart of listener, which is at other times zealously guarded by the vicious cobra of worldliness. It is Music Yoga that effortlessly brings about the Chitta-Vritti Nirodha of the Raja Yogi—control of mental modifications.

That Music, Sankirtan is an integral part of Bhakti Yoga it is needless to mention. Sankirtan and Bhakti are inseparable.

When thus, the mind is steadied and purified, and when the mind is merged in the Nada –all music is but the manifestation of the sacred Pranava or OM—the eye of intuition is opened and the Music Yogi gets Yoga-Siddhi or Samadhi.

What an inestimable service does he render to humanity! The true musician is the highest Nishkama Karma Yogi. He removes the sorrows of the people who listen to him. Music cures incurable diseases, dispels the gloom of ignorance, of wrong notions, and of despair from the heart, and instils in it joy, cheer, happiness and hope. You cannot easily repay the deep debt of gratitude you owe to the Music Yogi who renders you this inestimable service. It will earn for him the richest blessings of the Lord who will bestow upon him the highest reward of Atma-Jnana.

Such is the glory of this wonderful Music Yoga. Music is not an instrument for the titillation of the nerves or satisfaction of the senses; it is a Yoga Sadhana which enables you to attain Atma-Sakshatkara. It is the foremost duty of all musicians and institutions interested in the promotion of music to preserve this grand ideal and this pristine purity that belongs to music.

Saint Thyagaraja, Purandaradasa and others have repeatedly pointed this out, and by their own life of renunciation and devotion they have emphasised that music should be treated as Yoga and that true music can be tasted only by one who has renounced the world—freed himself from all taints of worldliness—and who practises music as a Sadhana for Self-realisation.

May their glorious example for ever inspire you all. May the Lord's richest blessings be showered on Sri Thyagaraja Sabha, and may the Sabha prosper from glory to greater glory and serve the people with the divine nectar of music! May God bless all the selfless workers of the Sabha with health, long life, peace, prosperity and Kaivalya Moksha!

SANKIRTAN YOGA

In this Kali Yuga, Vedanta and Kundalini Yoga are mere talks. They are not practicable for all ordinary aspirants. Vedanta demands gigantic will, deep enquiry and wonderful power of understanding and analysis. Very few possess these talents or faculties. For Kundalini Yoga one needs great spiritual vigour, absolute Brahmacharya for awakening Kundalini and taking it through the Chakras to the Sahasrara. These are more in theory. Practice is rather difficult.

So, in this Kali Yuga, Iron Age Sankirtan Yoga is the easiest, safest, cheapest and surest way for attaining God-realisation. Sankirtan and the practice of the formula, "Be good, do good'—this alone will give God-realisation. This alone can be practised by the vast majority of persons. Even those who practised Vedanta, have all come down to the practice of Sankirtan and Namasmaran, always remembering God. Even if there are breaks, it doesn't matter. We can have remembrance and eventually we will have uninterrupted remembrance like the bell-sound. You will have continuous remembrance and will rest in God. You will attain the super-conscious state which the Yogins enjoy.

You can study Kundalini Yoga and imagine that Kundalini is passing from Muladhara Chakra. It is some wind of acid passing through. Do not mistake it for Kundalini Sakti. Do Kirtan. Kundalini awakens itself and others' Kundalini also awakens. Kundalini can be easily awakened by chanting Divine Nam, Gurukripa, Guru Mantra, but of all these things Sankirtan Yoga is the best. Though Vedanta is good for talking and good for lectures, for a spiritual man Nam is very pleasing. He likes Japa. Nam strengthens. Nama is a great potential tonic. "Yajnanam Japayajnosmi." "Of all Yajnas I am Japa Yajna."

One who does Kirtan need not deliver lectures on Navavidha Bhakti, the nine modes of devotion. All Bhaktis or modes of devotion are in the singing of Kirtan. The veil of ignorance will be torn asunder by doing Kirtan.

They have prescribed Karma Yoga for removal of Mala or impurity, Upasana for removing Vikshepa or oscillation of the mind and meditation on Vedantic formulas for removing the veil of ignorance, Avarana. But Sankirtan removes all the three: Mala, Vikshepa and Avarana. That is the reason why Sankirtan is the best and easiest Yoga.

May all take to the practice of Sankirtan Yoga and attain the *summum bonum* of existence, viz. God-realisation, not tomorrow, but today, this very second!

MUSIC—THE EASIEST MEANS TO GOD-REALISATION

Music has the enchanting power of melting even stones. The effect of sweet tunes on some animals also, especially snakes and elephants, is no less than on human brings. Music is the most valuable means of upbringing the young. It adds to the character and leads ultimately to Happiness and God-realisation.

Appreciation of music by some very famous ancient authors says as follows:

गायते प्रियते देव:
सवग: पार्वतीपति:
गोपीपतिरनन्तोऽपि परं ध्वनिवरं गत:
सामगीतिरतो ब्रह्मा वीणा साक्षात् सरस्वती
प्रियन्ते यक्षगयवीदेवदानवमानवा:

Again the following quotations will tell you what it is, not to know, or at least understand and appreciate good music.

संगीतसाहित्यकलाविहीन:
साक्षात् पशु: पुच्छ्रविषाणहीन: ।
असौ वनं प्राप्य तृणं न भुङ्क्ते
तद् भागधेयं परमं पशूनाम् ॥

Shakespeare says:

"The man that hath no music in himself,
Nor is moved with concord of sweet sounds
Is fit for treasons, stratagems and spoils;
The motions of his spirit are dull as night,

(23)

And his affections, dark as Erabus:
Let no such man be trusted."

We find that from- primitive ages, most of the changes that have taken place in social, political, economic and religious conditions have been due to music and its enchanting powers.

Music has a very high educative value. It ennobles the mind, awakens and feeds the aesthetic sense and gives grace to all human expressions.

Fine arts are most essential to society. Every man and woman of some social standing should understand the aspects of those fine arts in which he or she is naturally gifted and personally interested. Music is one of the God-given gifts to humanity.

A composer can easily express his thoughts, through the medium of a song. It is one of the joys of humanity, and is the most harmless of pleasures. No art stirs emotions so deeply as music. Music is international and knows no barriers of religion, race, or creed or caste. It makes one forget himself and carries him into a sort of trance and helps him to enjoy Divine Ananda.

Even the great Saint Narada is believed to have been told by the Lord the following line:

नाहं वसामि वैकुण्ठे
योगिनां हृदये न वा ।
मद्भक्ता यत्र गायन्ते
तत्र तिष्ठामि नारद ॥

Meaning thereby:

"I dwell not in Vaikuntha (Heaven), nor in the hearts of Sages and Saints; but where my devotees sing, there I am, O Narada."

So, music is not a thing to be neglected or brushed aside. It must be a legitimate ambition of everyone, to be able to sing or play some instrument. Even Gods are moved by sweet music. Music gives peace and tranquillises our minds when we are agitated.

Any ordinary cultured person should have this power of appreciation inherent or cultivated. It is a wonderful art which gives relaxation to the troubled mind, strained nerves and develops the spirit of 'Bhakti Bhava'. Let us all try to serve God through our Divine Music.

The art or science of music is a means of shuffling of this mortal coil, and for enjoying a sacred pleasure while yet living.

It is said that no offerings can please God as much as the devotee's music.

It is the duty of everyone of us to lose no time to earn and keep this rare means with which to propitiate God and enter 'Vaikuntha,' the highest aim of life in this human birth.

Music is the essence of this universe and is the soul and the very breath of God. It is like the food for the appetite of the soul. It is a sacred science, its goal being God-Consciousness. Sangeeta Vidya is a holy and sacred science, which has a monetary gain. When a devotee sings with his intuitional and overflowing love of the Lord and the Guru, he realises God.   It is an instrument in the realisation of God. Music when clearly expressed with Rasa and Bhava, gives them the wisdom of Brahman, wherefrom arise the highest virtues of Peace and Patience.

Where is it that music is not wanted? In wars, in peace, in joy, in sorrow, in palaces and in Ashrams, everywhere it is welcomed. It has an expression of its own to suit the different occasions.

Music is the easiest, best and glorifying Sadhana to attain 'Moksha' in this age of Kali Yuga. One can enter into Bhava

Samadhi quite easily through devotional music. The music should emanate from the bottom of the heart simultaneously with sweet fervour and devotion. Music lulls, soothes and energises. Man wants music to relax and elevate him. The devotee sits with his Ektar, Tanpura, to melt his mind in his Lord in silence. Narada Rishi roams about in the three worlds with His Tanpura, singing Lord's Name. Music helps the devotee to commune with the Lord. It makes the mind one-pointed quickly." Music is Sangeet Yoga. It is an Anga of Bhakti Yoga. It is a Yoga Sadhana for God-realisation.

So, aspirants, start now itself with right earnest and practise music with your Bhakti Bhava and serve the Lord with your Divine Music and realise God in this very birth.

The cause of music must be served fairly and faithfully. No doubt that the All-India Radio is lifting up music to a great extent and making it more easily approachable. But that is not enough. More and more performances must be organised for the benefit of the vast public.

May God grant us all the courage and strength to prosecute the Divine Art and may we all be blessed through our Guru, to be worthy of God-realisation.

INDIAN MUSIC—A RETROSPECT

Man owes his knowledge, particularly in the realm of music to the inspiration that he drew from Nature. The singing bird, the whispering wind, the babbling brook and the buzzing bee, evoked in him an impulse of sympathetic imitation, and he took a further step in musical expression when he learnt to enjoy dance and singing in groups. The variety of pitch and tone in expressing moods and feelings must have led him to explore its possibilities as a vehicle of higher pursuits.

It was given to India to develop a scientific system of music long before the rest of the world woke up to civilisation. Illustrations of the 'Yazh', an ancient indigenous musical instrument resembling the harp, have been unearthed in Mohen-jo-daro. This points to the existence of a high standard of music in India five thousand years ago,

Indian music had its origin in the Vedas. It was the *Sama Veda* that gave the world the first full scale of seven notes. A device known as the Modal Shift of Tonic added to the number of full scales on one hand and led to the study of the intervals of pitch between note and note on the other. Scholars of music in ancient India thus came to discover the major tone, semi-tone and the quarter tone long ago. The process of evolution, doubtless, did cover a long period of slow, patient, arduous research and experiment. The untiring efforts of an unbroken line of great savants brought into existence a comprehensive scheme of full and minor scales.

Pythagoras formed the seven scales of the Greeks from Indian music. For centuries after, their musical output in Europe centred round them. But by and by, four of them went out of use and during the last four centuries all the music of Europe has been built round the remaining three known as the 'Gregorian

Chants'. In the 10th century A. D. an Italian Guido de Arezzo took the seven notes of the Indian scale, sa, ri, ga, ma, pa, dha, and ni and renamed them as Doh, ray, me, foh, soh, la, si, respectively. Ever since, the entire music of Europe has developed on the lines of harmony, polyphony, etc., while the keynote of Indian music is melody.

The impact of Muslim culture upon the music of India was great indeed. A robust, restless virile race, with a dynamic outlook on life and ideals, the Khilgis and the Moghuls of Delhi did their best to reconcile their iconoclastic impulse with an irresistible love for the ancient, noble arts of India. The inevitable result was that North India lost its old moorings and developed a system of music of its own, while South India entered a golden age of music. Only at the dawn of the present century, a great scholar of Maharashtra named Bhatkhande, took 10 out of the 72 scales of the South and into them he brought a large number of Ragas that floated without keel or anchor in the North.

When we review the contribution of music to the cultural, artistic and aesthetic life of India, we find that from time immemorial music has been linked with the religious life of the people. The temple and the Vihara fostered music, painting and sculpture as expressions of the yearning of the soul for the ultimate Beauty. Nataraja portrays the evolution of life by his cosmic dance. A host of heavenly beings are patron deities of music.

There is no secular music in India as it is commonly understood. For music always aimed at elevating life and making it noble and sweet. In fact, our composers have all been saints and seers who recorded their spiritual experiences in word and sound. Also there is an undercurrent of philosophy even in our folk songs.

Lasty, absolute music like the pure, melodic structure

known as Ragam and its complements, Tanam and Pallavi are features peculiar to Indian Music. Down through the ages they have been a perennial source of intellectual and aesthetic enjoyment even like the 'Moto Perpetuo' so beautifully rendered by the great violinist Yehudi Menuhin.

The effect of particular scales on the emotions and that of scales allotted to particular hours of the day are matters of absorbing interest. A number of temples in South India have pillars of resonant stone which are marvels of musical architecture. Music halls that carry sound without the aid of micro-phones may be found even to-day in South India, where the great civilisation of the Tamils brought about in the early centuries of the Christian era a remarkable synthesis of Aryan and Dravidian cultures. Also, more than 500 instruments of quality and refinement, many of them of resonant wood and even of stone, have enriched the music of India.

Our system of music is thus an ancient heritage of untold value and has provided the nucleus for all the music in the world today. May we cherish this precious fountain of culture and may it be given to us to guard it with vigilance and enrich it through our devoted service to the muse! In the cultural renaissance that is afoot in India I am confident Carnatic Music in northern India, will ultimately be a healthy meeting-ground for both the Carnatic and Hindustani systems of music and it will bring about a happy fusion of the two, enriching both.

Music is Nada Yoga. More urgent then even the achievement of technical perfection in Sangeeta and the enhancement of its melodic values, is the formation on the part of our musicians of the correct attitude towards this Vidya. In our country, music has always been regarded as Nadopasana or Yoga Sadhana, and never as food for the senses, however refined they may be.

Adepts in Yoga have recognised that there are vital centres

in the subtle body of man which vibrate and produce certain astral sounds. When certain Mantras are chanted or Kirtans sung, these inner vital-centres are influenced and the spiritual power latent in them is made manifest. This power enables the Nadopasaka—the spiritual aspirant who has made music his spiritual Sadhana—to get absolute control over his mind and the senses and thus to rise into the superconscious realms of Samadhi. When the mind attains Laya in Nada the mental modifications cease —and this is the aim of the Raja Yogi —and the Yogi gets into trance. This is the goal of Yoga; and this is the goal of Nadopasana. I pray to all the musicians of today to remember this all-important factor. They have the best instrument with which they can make rapid spiritual progress and attain the Goal of life—God-realisation—in this very birth.

The therapeutic aspect of music should engage the attention of the worthy leaders of the Sangeetha Sabhas. The Nada Yoga Mandirams should also undertake to serve humanity as a Healing Centre. Indeed, the very music that would constantly resound in the Mandirams would heal the body, mind and soul of all those who take part in the activities of the Sabhas. I hope that the Sabhas will encourage the study of this branch of music and undertake the music-treatment of man's maladies. Thus would Karma Yoga, Bhakti Yoga and Jnana Yoga all be combined into this grand Nada Yoga, leading its practitioners through this integral Sadhana, to the Supreme State of Final Liberation.

LORD KRISHNA'S FLUTE

Krishna's Flute is the symbol of freedom or Pranava. He has preached Prema through His Flute. He has created this world out of the Dhwani Omkara that emanates from His Flute. He stands on the right big toe. This signifies the Upanishadic utteranace: *Ekam eva'dviteeyam brahma*—"One without a second." He shows three curves while standing. This represents the three Gunas by which He has created this world. He gazes at Radha and puts the Prakriti in motion. He is the *primum mobile*. The lotus on which He stands, represents the universe.

Once Radha asked Krishna: "O my dear! Why do you love the Flute more than me? What virtuous actions has it done, so that it can remain in close contact with your lips? Kindly explain to me, my Lord, the secret of this, I am eager to hear." Krishna replied: "This Flute is very dear to me. It has got some wonderful virtues. It has emptied itself of its egoism before I began to play. It has made its inside quite hollow and I can bring out any kind of tune, Raga or Ragini, to My pleasure and sweet will. If you also behave towards Me in exactly the same manner as this Flute, if you remove your egoism completely and do perfect self-surrender, then I shall also love you in the same manner as I love this Flute."

This body also is the Flute of Lord Krishna in the macrocosm. If you can destroy your egoism and do total self-surrender, unreserved Atma-nivedan to the Lord, He will play on this body-flute nicely and bring out melodious tunes. Your will will become merged in His will. He will work unhampered through your instruments—body, mind and Indriyas. You can rest very peacefully then without care, worry or anxiety. You can watch the play of the universe as a Sakshi. Then your Sadhana will go on by leaps and bounds, because the

Divine Will or the Divine Grace itself will work through you. In fact, you need not do any Sadhana at all. But do the self-surrender from the very core of your heart with all your being (Sarvabhavena). Learn the lesson from the Flute and follow its ways. If you have done complete Saranagati at the Lotus-Feet of Lord Krishna, you have already reached the goal, you have already attained the realm of Peace, the Kingdom of Immortality, the domain of Eternal Bliss and Everlasting Sunshine. You have found out a joy that never fades, a life that never decays nor dies. You have reached the other shore of fearlessness, which is beyond darkness, despair, doubt, grief, sorrow, pain and delusion.

Purify your mind. Destroy your evil Vasanas and egoism. Hear once more the Flute of the Bansiwala Banke-Bihari of Brindavan, His Immortal Song of the Gita and allow Him to play in this body-flute of yours. Lose not this rare opportunity. It is very difficult to get again this human body.

Call Him fervently with single-minded devotion and purify and sing this song of welcome. He will surely appear before you.

> "He Krishna aja bansi baja ja
> He Krishna aja gita sunaja
> He Krishna aja makkhan khaja
> He Krishna aja lila—dikhaja."

THE SECRET OF MOHAN MURALI

Gopis (enviously addressing Murali): *"Ye sakhi murali!* Tell us the truth. Please do not keep it a secret. What merits does our Lord see in thee that He holds you so lovingly and tenderly day and night that you might drink deep the nectar of His lovely lips—the special possession of ours, the Gopis—and instals thee as the most beloved queen amongst us all? Wherein lies the charm, the beauty, the grace and attractiveness in thee ? Will you not reveal that secret to us, the constant beggars of Krishna's Love? Though black and born of a wild bamboo family, thou hast bewitched our Lord! When He plays upon you, the peacock madly dances to your tunes, and other birds stand dumb on the summit of the hills. Even the most dreadful cobra is humbled and becomes spell-bound. We all (i.e., the Gopis) lose our normal consciousness and hurriedly wear our nose rings in the ears and the earrings in the nose to meet Him. The cows give up their cudding and the calves their sucking and stand like statues with ears erect and rapt attention. Ah! How alluring is the melody of thy music! It seems you are not Murali but a magic wand. Thy music is as if the spiritual bliss materialised. It attracts and holds the Jivas and their roaming Vrittis in supreme and solemn peace of Brahma. Lulled by thy melodies, they are lost in the Supreme Self devoid of all personality. It is as if the Anahat Nada, the inner unceasing sound of Yogins, externalised. Hail Sakhi Bansi! Today we won't leave you until you intimate us into thy bosom secrets."

Murali (gently smiling): "My dear friends! I know neither magic nor any arts of attraction. I do not possess any merits also. Dead ignorant of them all, I am a simple forest-reed, all hollow within and bereft of any beauty. Krishna, my Lord, Lover and Bearer, calls this attitude of mine the greatest virtue, and is

(33)

extremely pleased with it. He over and over again whispers into my ear-hole this excellent axiomatic Upadesha: EMPTY THYSELF AND I WILL FILL THEE. I have realised its truth, and I obey it to the very letter. This is magic, if magic you will call it. This is my strength. It is He who sings through me and enchants you all. My dear friends! If you too empty yourselves of all the arrogant airs of your beauty, excellence, family pride, and possession; He will fill every nerve and atom of your body with His Love and Life. Does the pervading air not fill a jar, when it is emptied of other impeding stuffs ? He will not leave you even for a moment, I tell you, and will ever sing through you the sweet soothing melodies of harmony and peace to the whole world.

As I understand, every creature here is His flute or Bansi, the instrument of expressing His divine voice. You too are His Murali. The sockets or seats of organs in the body such as eyes, ears, etc., are his blow-holes. He blows through them various notes. To talk poetically, he sings sweet melodies through your tongue, beauties through your eyes and fragrance through your nose and so on. Every heart is Madhubana, the seat of all his Lilas, the rendezvous of all the Gopis, the centre of all the Vrittis. There the only Purusha is Sri Krishna. All others have to make a passive surrender to HIM

All the sounds is His Voice: Para, Pashyanti, Madhyama and Vaikhari are the various gradations of sound. They are the gradual and materialised expressions of his voice. (To give a slight idea of them: Vaikhari is well known to us. It needs no description. Madhyama is the intermediate unexpressed state of sound. Now Pashyanti is this: The clairvoyants say that the sound is associated with colour and form and accordingly the Pashyanti state of a word is an object of internal vision. This is the reason why it is named Pashyanti. The more we trace the inner origin of different languages, we are approaching the vibratic homogeneity of sound behind them. Birds, beasts, Indians, Africans, Americans—all in Pashyanti state of His voice experience the same Bhavana of a thing. As one and the same Shakti working through ears, becomes hearing, through the eyes, becomes seeing, and so forth, so also the same Pashyanti Bhavana assumes different forms of sound when materialised. As gesture, being a sort of mute subtle language, it is one and the same for all persons. Any individual of any country, when thirsty would do the same gesture of holding his hand to his mouth in a certain typical manner. God or Ishwar with the help of his Mayaic power incarnates Himself first as Para Vani in the Muladhara Chakra, then materialises himself as Pashyanti in the Manipura Chakra at the navel, then as Madhyma and then eventually as Vaikhari. This is the divine descent of His voice).

He as Paratpara the transcendental, stands beyond and above all the bodies, Koshas and the states of consciousness and sound and from there with a mere will sets the vibrations of sound in motion to extend them on to the grosser planes. To us on the physical plane, this divine voice of His is known as Vaikhari or the physical speech. This is our Lord Krishna's blowing of the flute. The most inward minded can hear that inner voice and feel His divine being. Close your eyes. Withdraw the Indriyas and concentrate. After Long and constant practice, the voice will become audible to you. First retire into perfect seclusion and silence. Try to hear it alone on the beach of the roaring sea, on the high peak of a mountain, in the dead silence of dark starry nights, in a dense forest or a lonely cave, and then try to hear it within yourself when you command good concentration. Retain this experience and try to hear the voice in the busy hours of your daily life as well.

Purity of Heart, an imperative Necessity: Heart is naturally pure. It is made up of the Sattwic portion of the five elements but like the pure waters of a lake, its purity and transparency is ruffled and muddled with our crude and earthly attractions and repulsions and such other pairs of opposites. Thus the free passage through which the vibrations of his voice are streaming forth is blocked, as it were, and like the clogged and roughly handled reeds of a harmonium, begins to emit discordant notes of envy and anger, hatred and censure, and so forth. Then it is said that we do not allow the inner Lord Krishna to blow uninterrupted the Bansi of our hearts. Therefore, my friends, keep your heart ever unalloyed and pure and the Lord within will be highly pleased to manifest His voice through you. Then ambrosial words will be dripping from your lips and your talk will mesmerise and magnetise the people with its modesty, respect and love. Their woes and sorrows will be washed away. Your word will not go unheard. Nobody will have strength to contradict your opinion. Your speech will be a Murali to them. Your word will soothe thousands of wounded and bleeding hearts and radiate joy and peace. Thus, my friends, purity of heart expresses the divinity of His voice. But how will you know that your heart is getting purer?

Thermometer to guage Heart-purity: By the words a person utters, the purity of his mind can be estimated. A person of pure heart has the innocent, straightforward nature of a child, and his actions are harmless and devoid of any deception to others. Cheerfulness is another form of purity. Sri Sankaracharya says in his Viveka-Chudamani: "When ignorance, negligence, silliness, stupidity and dullness prevail, you should understand that the heart is overshadowed by inertia while envy, anger, desire, avarice, hypocrisy, arrogance, etc , indicate that the heart is filled with Rajas or emotional agitating matter. And modesty, morality, faith, devotion to God, selflessness, control of Indriyas and intense desire for liberation are indicative of the increase of Sattwa (purity). And cheerfulness, experience of the soul, perfect peace, satisfaction, joy and stability of faith in God or Atman are associated with the perfection of purity."

The Means to Purity: Charity, disinterested service of the poor and the distressed, Japa, Kirtan, love, devotion, offering every good thing to God, austerities, discrimination of the real from the unreal, desirelessness; disinterested Guru-Bhakti, idea of God or Atman in all beings, Yama, Niyama, withdrawal of the senses and the mind from sensual objects, concentration, meditation on God, Atman or OM and many other means are prescribed according to the taste, capacity and temperament of the individual.

The Jnanis purify their hearts by the practice of Neti, Neti (not this, not this—or Atman is something other than this), and the method of Naham (not I but He is in the body), while the Bhaktas or Bhagawatas by means of Dasoham attitude (ever I am His humble servant). Thereby all the undesirable matter of Rajas and Tamas or emotion and inertia is gradually expelled from the heart and as a result the Divine Bliss freely flows out to the world.

The Anahat-Nada: Due to deep concentration the Munis and Yogis hear this sweet, ever-musical sound within their own bodies. "Hearing My sound, as a deer is entrapped into a net, similarly their mind gets attached to the Anahat sound, forgets everything else, and leaves all roaming about here and there."

The Hamsa-Upanishad declares the same experience. There it is given that when Hamsa Mantra (Hamsa means "I am He") is repeated one crore of times with faith and Bhavana, varieties of Nada (sound) are heard. They are of ten sorts: A subtle and minute sound or Nada, sound of a big bell, sound of a conch or a Vina (an Indian lute) of a bell-metal, of a flute, of a kettle-drum, of a tabor (Mridanga) and of a rattling sound. The Divine Voice is thus expressed to our lower planes. Now let us go to another sort of His voice.

The Music of the Spheres: The music of the spheres is created by the rotation of the whole universe—the earth, moon, sun, stars, satellites, etc. Like the sweet humming sound of a top set in brisk motion, all the above-mentioned bodies similarly rotate on their own axis and thereby the music of the spheres is created. This, too, is His voice. Though inaudible to human ears, it does exist all the time and everywhere. Munis and Yogins can hear it. Having a simple receptive heart like receptive radio, I can catch the subtle vibrations of that universal sound. A properly arranged apparatus of any musical instrument can derive and deliver it to our physical world, as a milking apparatus milks the existing milk from a cow.

As He is controlling my blow-holes, allowing only those to remain open which give out the sweet charming notes from them, let Him similarly govern your Indriyas, mind and intellect as He likes. Let His will be done. Be completely resigned to Him, my friends, so that He might shine through your eyes, speak through your tongue and smell through your nostrils and so on. Both of you cannot be accommodated in one heart.

Merge Thy little self into the Supreme Self. Give up all ideas of agency. Don't say " I am the doer and enjoyer." Say once more along with me: "Oh Lord! I am a Murali Thine, blow me as you will, a puppet in Your hands, simply to act as You will." Sing then my brothers, in one unanimous voice.

VOICE FIGURES

The first manifestation of God is Ether or Sound. Sound is the Guna or quality of Ether. Sounds are vibrations. They give rise to definite forms. Each sound produces a form in the invisible world and combinations of sound create complicated shapes.

The textbooks of science describe certain experiments which show that notes produced by certain instruments trace out on a bed of sand definite geometrical figures. It is thus demonstrated that rythmical vibrations give rise to regular geometrical figures.

The Hindu books on music tell us that various musical tunes Ragas and Raginis have each a particular shape which the books graphically describe. For instance the Megha Raga is said to be a majestic figure seated on an elephant. The Basanta Raga is described as a beautiful youth decked with flowers. All this means that the particular Raga or Ragini, when accurately sung, produces aerial etheric vibrations which create certain characteristic shapes.

This view has recently received corroborations from the experiments carried on by Mrs. Watts Hughes, the gifted author of " Voice Figures." She recently delivered an illustrated lecture before a select audience in Lord Leighton's studio to demonstrate the beautiful scientific discoveries on which she has alighted as the result of many years of patient labour.

Mrs. Hughes sings into a simple instrument called an "Eidophone " which consists of a tube, a receiver and a flexible membrane, and she finds that each note assumes definite and constant shape, as revealed through a sensitive and mobile medium. At the outset of her lecture, she placed tiny seeds upon the flexible membrane and the air vibrations set up by the notes, she sounded, danced them into definite geometric patterns. Afterwards she used dusts of various kinds, lycopodium dust being found particularly suitable. A reporter describing the shapes of the notes, speaks of them as remarkable revelations of geometry, perspective and shading. "Stars, spirals, snakes, wonders in wheels and imagination rioting in a wealth of captivating methodical designs" such were what were shown first.

Once when Mrs. Hughes was singing a note, a daisy appeared and disappeared, and "I tried" she said, "to sing it back for weeks before, at last I succeeded." Now she knows the precise inflections of the particular note, that is a daisy, and it is made constant and definite by a strange method of coaxing and alteration of crescendo and diminendo. After the audience had gazed enrapped, a series of daisies, some with succeeding rows of petals and some with petals delicately viewed, they were shown other notes, and these were pandies of great beauty. "How wonderful, how lovely" were the audible exclamations, that arose in the late Lord Leighton's studio, and exquisite form succeeded exquisite forms on the screen. The flowers were followed by sea-monsters, serpentine form of swelling rotundity, full of light and shade and detail, feeding in miles of perspective. After these notes came others and there were trees, trees with fruits falling, trees with a foreground of rocks, trees with sea behind, "Why" exclaimed people in the audience, they are just like Japanense landscapes.

While in France, Madame Finlang's singing of a hymn to Virgin Mary "O Ave Marium" brought out the form of Mary with child Jusus in her lap and again the singing of a hymn to 'Bhairava' by a Bengali student of Banaras (India) studying in France, gave rise to the formation of the figure of Bhairava with his vehicle dog.

Thus the repeated singing of the Name of the Lord gradually builds up the forms of the Devatas or the special manifestations of the deity, whom you seek to worship and this serves as a focus to concentrate the benign influence of the Being, which radiating from the centre, penetrates the worshipper of the singer or Sangeeta-Premi.

When one enters the state of meditation, the inner Vritti-flow is greatly intensified. The deeper one goes into meditation the more marked is the effect. The concentration of the mind upwards sends a rush of this force through the top of the head and the response comes in a fine rain of soft magnetism. This feeling arising from the downward power sends a wonderful glow through the body, and one feels as though bathed in a soft kind of electricity.

The above experiments demonstrate the following facts:-

1. Sounds produce shape.

2. Particular notes give rise to particular forms.

3. If you want to reproduce a particular form, you must recite a particular note in a particular pitch.

4. That, for that purpose no other note and no other pitch, chanting even the identical note will avail. For instance in *'Agnimile purohitam'* — *'Ile Agnim purohitam'* will not do. In doing so, the efficacy of the Mantra is gone. You cannot therefore transpose or translate a Mantra. If you do it, it will cease to be a Mantra. When a Mantra is defective either in Svara or Varna, it is incorrectly directed and may produce a result just contrary to what was intended.

But such is not the case with Rama Nama or any Name of the Lord, viz., Siva, Krishna or Hari, etc. These Names may be sung in any and every way.

> *"Ulta nama japat jaga jana,*
> *Valmiki bhaye brahma samana."*

All the world knows that Saint Valmiki (previously known as Rogue Ratnakara) became one with Brahma (the Lord) by uttering even the Ulta Nama—Mara, Mara, for Rama, Rama.

Rama Nama japate raho, Rijh bhajo ya khijh
Ulta pulta oopaje jasa dharti ko bija.

Therefore repeat the name of the Lord. Repeat it either in love (with feeling and Bhav or in anger), it will have its proper effect ; just as the seeds must sprout and grow, either sown properly or thrown into the fields in whatever way, the peasant pleaseth to do.

Sangeeta is an exact science. The harmonious vibrations produced by the singing of the Names of Lord help the devotee to control his mind easily. They produce benign soothing influence on the mind. They elevate the mind at once from its old ruts or grooves to a magnanimous heights of divine splendour and glory.

MUSICO-THERAPY

Music is an aid to treatment of diseases. In America doctors are treating patients who are suffering from nervous diseases through music (musico-therapy). In ancient Egypt music was used in temples in healing diseases of the nervous class.

Sages affirm that many diseases can be cured by the melodious sound of a flute or violin or vina or saranghi. They maintain that there is an extraordinary power of music over diseases.

Harmonious rhythm caused by sweet music has attractive property. It draws out disease. The disease comes out to encounter the music wave. The two blend together and vanish in space.

Music soothes the brain and the nerves. It lulls the whole system. It stimulates, energises, invigorates, galvanises and vitalises the whole system. It affects the emotions and arouses the impulses to action and thereby influences all the vital functions. It consists of a series of harmonious vibrations, electrical in their nature and make-up.

Music relaxes nervous tension and makes parts of the body affected by tension to resume their normal functions.

Music is highly beneficial in the treatment of nervous disorders, sleeplessness, etc.

Music has tremendous power to bring comfort and solace when one is in a state of despondency or pain.

Sangeeta or Kirtan is the best medicine and tonic when all other systems of medicine have failed to cure a disease. Kirtan will work wonders. Kirtan is the sole refuge and sheet-anchor in the treatment of chronic incurable diseases. Try this unique medicine and realise its marvellous benefits.

Sweet melody exercises a powerful influence on the mind and physical nature of every living being. Sangeeta or Kirtan destroys sins, purifies the heart and brings the Kirtanist face to face with God. If any one is suffering from any disease, do Kirtan near his bed. He will soon be cured of his disease.

BENEFITS OF SANGEETA

There are four kinds of sound, viz., Vaikhari (vocal) Madhyama (from the throat), Pashyanti (from heart) and Para (from navel). Sound originates from navel. Vedas also originate from navel. Sangeeta and Vedas are born from the same source.

God is a mystery. Mind is a mystery. The world is a mystery. How Sangeeta transmutes human nature into Divine Nature, how it overhauls the old vicious Samskaras, how it changes the mental substance, how it transforms or metamorphoses the asuric diabolical nature into pure Sattwic nature and how it brings the devotee face to face with God is also a mystery. Science and reason can hardly explain the *modus operandi* of Sankirtan. Reason is an imperfect instrument. A man of weak intellect can be defeated by one who has a stronger intellect. Reason cannot explain many life problems. Intuition transcends reason but it does not contradict reason.

There is a great Sakti in every word. The very uttering of "Hot Pakouri" brings saliva in the mouth. If you utter the word faeces, when a man is taking his meals, he will immediately vomit. When such is the case with ordinary words what to speak of the Names of God. Every Name of God is filled with various divine Sakties and nectar, Nama and Nami are inseparable. Nama is even greater than the Nami. Even in worldly experiences, the man dies but his name is remembered for a long time. Kalidas and Shakespeare, Valmiki and Tulsidas are remembered even now.

An objector says, "If I say 'Sugar Candy,' Sugar Candy,' can I get it ? How can I see God if I simply sing Rama Rama?" In the case of sugar candy: sugar candy is outside, but God resides in the very chamber of your heart. He is close to you. By repeating Rama Rama, the mind becomes one-pointed. It melts in silence, in the heart you get darshan of God. The knower of God is as good as God Himself. God is Chaitanya and so is His Name. It is not so with other objects or names of objects.

Name of the Chaitanya (Atma), even of the human being is ever the same. There is a man in sound sleep, the Pranas are there in and with him. He will not hear you, if you call on him addressing 'Prana or Apana.' Just call him by his name Rama or Shyama, he will hear you and will get up from his sleep. Such is the power of Nama. Nama is nothing but Chaitanya personified.

'Sangeeta' breaks the three Granthies or knots of ignorance: Brahma Granthi, Vishnu Granthi and Rudra Granthi. It purifies the Nadies (Nadi Shuddhi) and the Pranamaya-Kosha (vital sheath) and easily, awakens the sleeping Kundalini that is coiled up in Muladhara Chakra and eventually brings on divine ecstatic mood (Bhava-Samadhi). It produces Ekagrata Chitta (onepointed mind), purifies the chitta (Chitta Shuddhi), destroys all Vasanas, Trishna (cravings), Kamanas, Chapalta, Sankalpas and all sorts of whims, moods, fancies and wild imaginations. It destroys the three Doshas (faults) viz., Mala, Vikshepa and Avarna (impurites), tossing of mind and veil of ignorance. It annihilates the three kinds of Tapas (fevers) Adhyatmic, Adhibhoutic and Adhidaivic. It eradicates the five Kleshas (afflictions) viz., Avidya (ignorance), Asmita (egoism), Ragadwesha (love and hatred) and Abhinivesa (clinging to life) and also Janma, Mrityu, Jara, Vyadhi and Dukha (birth, death, old age, sickness and miseries). It destroys the three kinds of Karmas, viz., Sanchita (accumulated), Prarabdha (fruitiscent), Agami or Kriyamana (current actions). It destroys Rajas and Tamas and fills the mind with Sattwa (purity). The mind is more concentrated on the melodious Dhwani (sound) and gets Laya (dissolution or involution) soon. Just as the snake is charmed by sweet melodious sound, so also the snake-mind is charmed by sweet melodious Dhwani of Sangeeta.

He who does Sangeeta forgets the body and the world, Sangeeta removes Dehadhyasa (identification with the body). It brings Super-intuitional knowledge. Tukaram was an agricultural peasant. He could not even sign his name. He was always doing Sankirtan of Lord Sri Krishna's Name "Vithala, Vithala" with cymbals in his hands. He had Darshana of Lord Krishna in physical form. His inner-sight (Jnana Sakti) —Divya-dristi was opened by Sankirtan. His inspiring Abhangas are texts for M.A. students of the Bombay University. Wherefrom did the unlettered Tuka derive his knowledge? He tapped the fountain of knowledge through Sankirtan. He penetrated into divine source through Bhava-Samadhi; that was brought about by deep Sankirtan. Does this not clearly prove that God exists, that the Swarup of God is knowledge, and that Sankirtan has tremendous influence?

The first manifestation of God is Ether or Sound. Sound is the Guna or quality of Ether. Nagar-kirtan purifies the Ether, air, water, and earth. When the earth is purified, you will have abundant crops, Aushadhies will grow exuberantly.

Sangeeta purifies the surging, evil lower emotions and fills the mind with sublime soul-elevating higher emotions. It destroys the mind " Mano-nasa," and brings about thoughtless state. Practise, try; fill yourself. Just as the intoxication that you get by taking a dose of opium or *cannabis indica*, lasts for some hours, during the following day also, during Kirian, a spiritual wave comes from the Indweller of your heart and purifies the mind and Pranamaya-kosha. At night you will be free from bad dreams. All diseases are cured thereby. Doctor's bills will be saved. Just as oil flows from one vessel to another vessel, Sattwa flows from the Lord to your mind.

Sangeeta gives you the strength to face the difficulties in the battle of life. Singing the Names of the Lord is a mental tonic. A strong habit of singing the names of the Lord will be formed in six months. Even when anyone is in a dying state, the habit of singing the Name of Lord will come to the rescue at the last moment.

NADA UPASANA

There are Upanishads which are words of experienced wisdom which deal about Nada Upasana and there is a whole Upanishad on the Pranava and there is a masterpiece, viz: Gaudapadacharya's Karika on Mandukyopanishad.

Bhava, Raga and Tala—all these three have to go in harmonious combination to produce the desired result. Even stones can be melted by music. The Tandava of Ravana could melt the stones of Mount Kailas. The philosophy of music ultimately is that which we find running throughout the Vedas. There is no need for us to worry how many—twenty five or more—principles are there. Here even a Tangawala repeats OM.

Nada Yoga kills the Tapatrayas, controls the senses, tames the mind and enables one to attain the knowledge of the Self. The quickest and surest way to attain God is melody. Shakespeare says, "The man who is not moved by the concord of sweet sounds is fit for treasons, stratagems and spoils...Let no such man be trusted."

Music can sometimes cure *incurable diseases*. It can soothe the brain and the nerves. Householders get despondency sometimes. When they repeat the Name of the Lord, they become cheerful. Maha Vaidyanathier cured by his music the dire stomach-ache of Namachivaya Thampiran.

Sangeeta pleases the ear, is a rich treat to the senses and the mind, in fact, so much so that the senses and the mind are tamed and controlled by it; and Sangeeta ennobles the soul and reveals the Self within. Music brings about Vasanakshaya. The vertebral column is the inspirer of Veena. The Kundalini should be roused through melodies sung by expert people; otherwise it will lead to undesirable results.

Thyagaraja attained Darshan of Sri Rama through music. St. John writes, "In the beginning there was the word and the word was God." From far off times human beings could hear this divine sound. Ravana, Tulsidas, Tukaram, Ekanath and Saint Thyagaraja attained Realisation through Sankirtan. The symphony produced by Bhava, Raga and Tala will melt even stones.

In the experiments that are here expounded with devotion and humility in the atmosphere of selflessness we know that Sangeeta Yoga has got a proper place. If the *hridayakamala* can be melted through Sankirtan, we can merge ourselves in the *Hridayakamalavasin*.

MUSIC COLOURS AND SCENTS

The life-force comes down to us through the ether in forms of vibrations. We speak of the great octave of cosmic vibrations, because the entire vibrations are in correspondence or sympathy like the tunes of the octave in music. If for instance, the low 'SI' or 'DO' is struck the higher 'SI' or DO's will vibrate or sound simultaneously in sympathy. On the lower end of the octave vibration stand sounds which are the lowest of them. The human ear can perceive from 16 to roughly 30,000 vibrations per second. Some animals like dogs can hear even higher tunes. Much higher in the scale of vibrations stand colours. Each of the seven colours corresponds to one of the seven tunes. Still higher in the scale of vibrations stand perfumes or scents, the other forms of vibrations being electricity, heat, X-rays, ultraviolet rays, cosmic rays.

All these vibrations penetrate our astral body and work on it creating either harmonious or disturbing feelings. Everybody knows that certain surroundings and certain tunes produce harmony and joy in us whilst others irritate and depress.

The old Egyptians knew the art of constituting harmony in a diseased person in leading him in a stretcher into a temple where a clairvoyant priestess simply could see the astral body and the health aura of the patient and submitted him to creating colours and tunes which were beneficial for breaking down the wrong vibrations which were the source of the disease.

It is nowadays a common experience that in certain moods we are drawn to a certain music which gives us peace, also that we like to wear certain clothes or furnish our rooms or paint our walls with certain colours which have a beneficial influence on the happiness and health of the person. Whereas the reasons and rules of these influences are mostly unknown to the average man, the occult can know the influences of these different vibrations. They therefore can advise which of these manifestations of vibrations should be applied or used in each case.

Colour healing is used already in many cases, even in hospital, and treatment by music has given good results in some lunatic asylums. In New York, in one of the busiest streets an experiment was made in a hall of which the walls were painted with nerve soothing colours and that the by-passers could sit in that hall for a certain time in silence and feel the calming influence of that surrounding in their nervous system.

"Music whilst you work" which is nowadays applied in most factories of the Western world, has its origin in the experience that the workers will work better if they are under the influence of certain music whilst they work. Naturally the abuse of this system has led in most places to the phenomenon that after a certain time one does not hear any more the music which is not dosed in right quantity and in the right tunes.

Experiments in America mainly have shown that there exist correspondences between tunes, colours and perfumes, so that the vibration of one tune would set into vibration a colour and a perfume in the higher scale of vibrations.

Hereafter I am giving the table of correspondences as established by Roland Hunt in his research in America.

Colour	Nervous Reaction	Musical Note	Perfume
Red	Stimulates, but quickly fatigues.	C	Camphor, Geranium, Sandalwood.
Orange	Stimulates, with tonic effect, cheerful and forceful.	D	Vanilla, Clematis, Heliotrope, Almond.

Yellow	Mental activity and clear thinking.	E	Jasmine, Cassia, Citron, Iris.
Green	Balance, relaxation and harmony.	F	Musk, Benzoin, Narcissus.
Blue	Healing and soothing.	G	Syringa, Lilac, Frangipani, Sweet Pea.
Indigo	Inspiration and self-control.	A	New Mown Hay, Lavender, Balsam.
Violet	Peace and calm. Higher plane healing	B	Carnation, Menthol, Peppermint, Cinnamon.

From this we can see what great possibilities are open in future by using all the three constituents, notes, colours and perfumes for producing a deep effect in a case of disease.

The Russian composer, Scriabine, has also done some pioneer work in this field in constructing a colour organ in which each tune was joined to its corresponding colour and would produce this colour whilst the music was played. He died, however, before his work was completed. Paul Disney has also impressed the world audiences by his film "Fantasia" in which he used music colours and thought forms.

It is to be hoped that when more study has been given to the subject, there may be established colour centres in every large town and doctors will rely mainly on colour, sound and perfume therapy instead of drugs for treatment of disease, and, what is far more important, for the maintenance of health. When we remember that disease is really a vibratory disorder, surely we are justified in thinking that medicine will develop along these lines or as Marconi remarked, "We are just entering what may be called the field of vibrations, a field in which we may find more wonders than mind can conceive."

NRITYA: A DIVINE SCIENCE

No man is an absolute male and no woman is an absolute female. There is always a mixture of masculine and feminine qualities in both. There are some males in whom the feminine elements are predominant. Examples are many in the world. Even so no man is absolutely emotional. There is a mixture of both. One may be more rational and in him the faculty of reason may be more developed, and the other may be more emotional and in him the heart may be more developed.

Some foolish dry Vedantins who pose themselves as "Advaita Vadins", dislike Sankirtan and speak ill of Sankirtan and Nritya. Swami Rama Tirtha, a fine example of ideal Vedantin, danced in the Brahma-puri forests, when he was in divine ecstatic mood with *ghunghru* tied to his feet. He had a harmonious combination of head and heart. Lord Gouranga was another genius. He was master of Nyaya (Logic). He also did Nritya and Sankirtan. He developed his head and heart.

Nritya is an exact science. Nritya is Adhyatmic and celestial. The founders of this blessed science are Lord Krishna and Lord Siva. You will have to exhibit the six Bhavas in your Nartanam (dance). These are—Utpatti (creation), Vinasam (destruction), Gati (movement), Agati (stability), Vidya (knowledge) and Avidya (ignorance).

Nritya that accompanies a Kirtan is an inseparable, sacred movement of the various limbs of the body in accordance with the inner divine Bhav.

Nritya is a divine science. Those who do Nritya should bring out the six Bhavas. It is an external manifestation induced in Bhaktas by the thrill of ecstasy from within and helps the devotees in merging themselves in the Lord.

(54)

Supreme joy and magnanimity of the sacred Nritya could only be understood by Rishis and devotees like Narada, Vyasa, Suka, Mira, Tukka, Gouranga, Hafiz and others and not by the worldly-minded persons whose minds are saturated with passion.

The Adi Gurus for this celestial Nritya were Lord Siva, Krishna and Mother Kali. Dancing that accompanies vulgar music and obscene songs with intoxicants is invariably the outcome of passion and base thoughts. It has a deep tinge of lust. Do you see clearly the difference now, friends?

Mark, how Lord Krishna stands with Flute in His hands showing these six Bhavas.O dry, one-sided Vedantins! Give up cavilling. Learn to be wise. Give up dry, idle talking. Develop your head, heart and hands and attain perfection. There is not an iota of hope for your salvation till you develop your heart. Dear friends, bear this in mind always.

THE POWER OF NRITYA

In the Lord's Supreme Dance, the universe had its origin: indeed, in it alone has the world its life: and finally, when the time comes, into His dance all this will be withdrawn.

Nritya creates, sustains and destroys. Preserved on the high pedestal of purity, sublimity and as an expression of the finest sentiments of the heart, this threefold process is at once divinised. Nritya will then create devotion in even a stony heart hardened by a subhuman pursuit of material pleasures ; Nritya will sustain the devotion of the dancers themselves and their life, too, as well as the life of all the spectators—Nritya is a life-giving tonic ; and Nritya will destroy—destroy all the evils that assail a man from within. For, it is lack of development of the heart that gives room for the growth of Evil; Nritya develops the heart and, therefore, annihilates Evil.

Lord Krishna was very fond of dancing. To please Him the Gopis would dance: the dance would make them forget themselves and lose themselves in Him. They lived in Him: and He lived in them! In recent times, Mira Bai took up this tradition. She danced her way into the heart of the Lord. Lord Gouranga danced along the roads, singing the Names of the Lord. The very sight of him could convert even confirmed rogues into perfect saints! In the many Sankirtan Conferences over which I have presided, held all over Northern India, all the participants used to dance in ecstasy—Sannyasins, Bhaktas, Yogis, all!

For, dancing is a part of Synthetic Yoga. It develops one's body, mind, heart and soul. The intellect of even the spectators is sharpened and subtilised when they try to follow the meaning of those rapid movements of the limbs and eyes! Dancing spreads its magic spell over all your faculties: it is a powerful aid to concentration. When the devotee feels the need of an aid to drive out extraneous thoughts from his mind, he takes to Nritya. Very soon he is filled with God! Such is the power of Nritya.

DANCE OF SIVA

The flood of nineteen-twenty-four
Was horrible in Rishikesh
It carried away many Mahatmas and Sadhus
This is the dance of Siva.

The impetuous Chandrabhaga
Turned its course in 1943
People crossed it with difficulty
With the help of elephant
This is the dance of Siva.

In the morning of eleventh January 1945
There was fall of snow
On the surrounding Himalayas.
The chill was terrible
This is the dance of Siva.

Lord Vishwanath dwells now
In a place where there was forest
He pleases the whole world
He bestows health and long life
This is the dance of Siva.

Forests become Ashrams
Islands become an ocean
Ocean becomes an Island
Cities become deserts
This is the dance of Siva.

Siva gazes at His Sakti
Then there is the atomic dance
There is the dance of Prakriti
Lord Siva merely witnesses
This is the dance of Siva.

Then Prana vibrates, mind moves
Senses function, Buddhi operates
Heart pumps, lungs breathe
Stomach digests, intestines excrete
This is the dance of Siva.

This is a world of change
A changing thing is perishable
Know the Imperishable
Which is changeless
And become Immortal.

PHILOSOPHY OF SIVA TANDAVA

I

पादस्याविर्भवन्ती मवनतिमवने रक्षत: स्वैरपातै:
संकोचेनैव दोष्णां मुहुरभिनयत: सर्वलोकातिगानाम् ।
दृष्टं लक्ष्यषु नोग्रेज्वलनकणमुचं बध्नतो दाह भीते-
रित्याधारानुरोधात् त्रिपुर विजयिन: पातु वो दु:खनृत्तम् ॥

The Tandava or celestial dance of Lord Siva is extremely thrilling and charming, exquisitely graceful in pose and rhythm and intensely piercing in effect.

Nritya or Tandava is an inseparable, sacred movement of the various limbs of the body in accordance with the inner divine Bhav.

The dance of Lord Siva is for the welfare of the world. The object of His dance is to free the souls from the fetters of Maya, from the three bonds of Anavamal, Karma and Mayamal. He is not the destroyer but He is the regenerator. He is the Mangal Data and Ananda Data, bestower of auspiciousness and bliss. He is more easily pleased than Lord Hari. He grants boons quickly, for a little Tapas or a little recitation of His five letters.

Aghad Bhum is His song of dance. When Siva starts His dance Brahma, Vishnu, the Siva Ganas and Kali with Her bowl of skull join Him. Have you not seen the picture of Pradosha Nritya? It will give you an idea of the dance of Siva.

Kali was very proud of her ability in dancing. Siva started dancing to quell Her pride. He danced very beautifully, very artistically. Kali had to put Her face down in shame.

Lord Siva wears a deer on the left upper hand. He has trident on the right lower arm. He has fire and Damaru and Malu or a kind of weapon. He wears five serpents as ornaments. He wears a garland of skulls. He is pressing with His feet the demon Muyalaka, a dwarf holding a cobra. He faces south. Panchakshari itself is His body. Lord Siva says, "Control the five senses which are hissing like serpents. The mind is jumping like a deer. Control the mind. Burn it in the fire of meditation. Strike it down with the rod of Trisula of discrimination. You can attain Me." This is the philosophical significance of the picture of Lord Siva.

You can witness the dance of Siva in the rising waves of the ocean, in the oscillation of the mind, in the movements of the senses and the Pranas, in the rotation of the planets and constellations, in cosmic Pralaya, in epidemics of infectious diseases, in huge inundations and volcanic eruptions, in earthquakes, landslips, lightning and thunder, in huge conflagrations and cyclonic storm.

As soon as the Guna Samya Avastha wherein the three Gunas exist in a state of equilibrium is disturbed by the will of the Lord, the Gunas manifest and quintuplication of elements takes place. There is vibration of Omkara or Sabda Brahman. There is manifestation of primal energy. This is the dance of Siva. The whole cosmic play or activity or Lila is the dance of Siva. All movements within the cosmos are His dance. He gazes on Prakriti and energises Her. Mind, Prana, matter begins to dance. When He begins to dance the Sakti Tattva manifests. From Sakti, Nada proceeds and from Nada, Bindu originates. Then the universe of names and forms is projected. The undifferentiated matter, energy and sound become differentiated.

The burning grounds are the abodes of Siva. Rudra is the destructive aspect of the Lord. Lord Siva dances in the crematorium with Kali in His ten-armed form. The Siva Ganas also join with Him in the dance.

Nataraja of Chidambaram is the expert dancer. He has four hands. He wears the Ganges and the crescent moon on his matted locks. He holds Damaru in his right hand. He shows Abhaya Mudra to his devotees with His raised left hand. The significance is 'O devotees, do not be afraid. I shall protect you all.' One left hand holds the fire. The other right hand points down on the Asura Muyalaka who is holding a cobra. He has raised the left foot in a beautiful manner.

The sound of the drum invites the individual souls to his feet. It represents Omkara. All the Sanskrit alphabets have come out of the play of the Damru. Creation arises from Damaru. The hand which shows Abhaya Mudra gives protection. Destruction proceeds from fire. The raised foot indicates Maya or illusion. The hand which points down shows that His feet are the sole refuge of the individual souls. Tiruakshi represents Omkara or Pranava.

Chidambaram is a sacred place of pilgrimage in south India. All the Tamil saints have sung hymns in praise of Nataraja. There is Akasa Lingam here which indicates that Lord Siva is formless and attributeless. The popular saying goes, He who dies in Benares with Ram Nam in his lips and heart attains salvation. He who remembers Arunachalam or Tiruvannamalai attains Mukti. He who gets Darshan of Nataraja attains final emancipation. Real Chidambaram is within the heart. Nataraja dances in the hearts of devotees who have burnt egoism, lust, hatred, pride and jealousy.

He dances quite gently. If He dances vehemently the whole earth will sink down at once. He dances with His eyes closed because the sparks from His eyes will consume the entire universe. The five activities of the Lord Panchakrityas, viz., Srishti (creation), Sthithi (Preservation), Samhara (destruction), Tirobhava (illusion) and Anugraha (grace) are the dance of Siva.

May you all comprehend the true significance of the dance of Siva. May you all dance in ecstasy in tune with Lord Siva and merge in Him and enjoy the Sivananda, the final beatitude of life.

PHILOSOPHY OF SIVA TANDAVA

II

Lord Siva is an embodiment of wisdom. He is the light of lights. He is Param-jyoti or supreme light. He is self-luminous or Swayam-jyoti. The dance of Siva represents the rhythm and movement of the world-spirit. At His dance the evil forces and darkness quiver and vanish.

In the night of Brahma or during Pralaya Prakriti is inert, motionless. There is Guna Samya Avastha. The three Gunas are in a state of equilibrium or poise. She cannot dance till Lord Siva wills it. Lord Siva rises from His profound silence and begins to dance. The undifferentiated sound becomes differentiated through the vibration set up by the movements of His Damaru or Drum. Sabda Brahman comes into being. The undifferentiated energy also becomes differentiated. The equipoise in the Gunas becomes disturbed. The three Gunas Sattva, Rajas and Tamas manifest. All the spheres, the atoms and the electrons also dance rhythmically and in an orderly manner. Atoms dance in the molecule and molecules dance in all bodies. Stars dance in time and space. Prakriti also begins to dance about Him as His glory or Vibhuti. The Prana begins to operate on Akasa or subtle matter. Various forms manifest. Hiranyagarbha or the golden egg or cosmic mind also manifests.

When the time comes Lord Siva destroys all names and forms by fire while dancing. There is stillness again.

This is the symbolism involved in the form of Nataraja. The deer in the hand of Siva represents Asuddha Maya. The axe represents knowledge which destroys ignorance. The drum, the outstretched arm that carries fire, the water (Ganga), the hand with the axe, the foot standing on the Asura Muyalakan are the formless or Sukshma Panchakshara.

Srishti (creation) is in the drum, Sthithi (preservation) is in the Abhaya hand that holds the axe; Tirobhava (veiling) is in the pressing foot; and Anugraha (or blessing) is in the uplifted foot.

There are various kinds of dances of Siva. There are the Samhara dance, the five dances, six dances, the eight dances, the Kodu Kotti dance, the Pandam dance, the Kodu dance. The Kodu Kotti is the dance after the destruction of everything. Padam is the dance after the destruction of the three cities, wearing the ashes of those cities. Kodu or Kapalam is the dance holding Brahma's head in the hand. Samhara is the dance at the time of disolution or Pralaya.

Srishti, Sthithi, Samhara, Tirobhava, and Anugraha and also Muni-Tandava, Anavarata Tandava and Ananda Tandava constitute the eight dances. Sivananda dance, Sundara dance, the golden city dance, the golden Chidambaram dance and the wonderful dance form the five dances. The five funitious dances and the Ananda dance in the end form the six dances.

Lord Siva is the only dancer. He is the Master or expert dancer. He is the King of dancers. He quelled the pride of Kali. Lord Siva's destruction is not a single act but is a series of acts. There is a different kind of dances at every stage.

May Lord Nataraja, the great dancer help you in the attainment of Sivanandam or the eternal bliss of Siva!

LORD NATARAJA—THE GREAT DANCER

'Ya' in 'Namah Sivaya' represents Jiva or the individual soul. The Panchakahara 'Namah Sivaya' forms the body of Lord Siva. The hand that wears fire is 'Na'. The foot that presses the demon Muyalaka is 'Ma'. The hand that holds Damaru is 'Si'. The right and left hands that move about are 'Va'. The hand that shows "Abhaya" is 'Ya'.

Once upon a time a group of Rishis abandoned their faith in the true Lord and took to the worship of false deities. Lord Siva wanted to teach them a lesson. He stirred in them strange passions. The Rishis became very furious. They created many evils through their power of penance and let them loose upon Siva. Lord Siva overcame, finally defeated the great Kali, a creation of the Rishis by the cosmic dance.

At the time of Sri Nataraj's dance Patanjali Rishi and Vyagrapada were witnessing the dance and enjoying it. They were standing on either side of the Lord. Even in paintings and sculpture of the Nataraja's Murti you will find the figures of Patanjali and Vyagrapada on either side of Nataraja. The lower part of the body of Vyagrapada will resemble that of tiger and the corresponding part of Patanjali that of the serpent.

The most wonderful dance of Nataraja is the Urdhva Tandava. In this dance the left leg is lifted up and toe points to the sky. This is the most difficult form of dance. Nataraja defeated Kali by this pose in dancing. Kali successfully competed with Nataraja in all other modes of dance. Nataraja while dancing lost His earring. He succeeded by means of His toe, in this form of dance in restoring the ornament to its original place without the knowledge of the audience.

Nataraja danced with his right leg lifted upwards. This is

the Gajahastha pose in dancing or Nritya. He danced continuously without changing His legs once.

There is another dance-pose of Siva on the head of an elephant. In this form Lord Siva is known as Gajasena Murti. At the foot of Lord Siva there is the head of an elephant-monster. Lord Siva has eight hands. He holds the trident, the drum and the nose in His three right hands. He holds the shield and the skull in his two left hands. The third left hand is held in Vismaya-pose.

Siva killed the elephant and used the skin as His garment. An Asura assumed the form of an elephant to kill the Brahmins who were sitting round the Linga of Viswanath in Benares absorbed in meditation. Lord Siva came out suddenly from the Linga and killed the elephant monster.

RASA AND RHYTHM

Bhav is the main basis of Rasa. The relish of eternal bliss which the devotee enjoys during his ecstatic state of Bhav Samadhi is called Rasa.

Rasa is of the essence of Lord Krishna. Rasa is the nectarine transcendental bliss. Lord Krishna is the repository of fountain-source of Rasa.

Taste the Krishna-Bhakti Rasa through Rati or Prem and attain immortality.

Night follows day, light follows darkness; rest follows motion; this is the rhythm in Nature.

Harmony follows disharmony, peace follows war; calm follows storm; this is the rhythm in Nature.

Evolution follows involution; Pralaya follows creation; inhalation follows exhalation; this is the rhythm in Nature.

Birth follows death; pain follows pleasure; contraction follows expansion; this is the rhythrm in Nature.

Who is behind this rhythm? Who maintains this rhythm? Find Him out, O Ram! He is God. He is the Inner Ruler. Harmony is Peace. Harmony is God.

RASA-LILA

The gist of the Rasa-lila is the essence of devotion (Para-bhakti) or oneness, the merging of the lover and the beloved. The secret of Rasa-lila is that men or women while remaining in the world and doing all sorts of activities can develop Krishna-prema and can realise God head at their very threshold. It teaches; "Give the mind to God just as Radha did, and the hands to work. Sing. Dance in Divine Ecstasy."

In the esoteric sense heart itself is Brindavan. Mind is Radha. Gopies are the nerves and the Indriyas. Anahat sounds emanating from the heart are the melodious songs that come out of Krishna's Flute. Sahasrara-chakra is the Param Dhama. Lord Krishna is Para-Brahman. The five Koshas are the five fortresses. Pranas are the gatekeepers. Shad-chakras are the gates. Immortality is the Yamuna. The crown of the head is Kadamba tree. Mind melts in Brahman. Radha is united with Krishna. This is Rasa-lila.

THE SPIRITUAL BASIS OF BHARATA NATYAM

"The Alaripu"

The glorious Bharata Natyam Vidya and the tradition of Nritya in Bharatavarsha form one of the approaches to divinity through art. It is a deeply significant Sadhana for the realisation of God through the avenue of Kala. This spiritual basis underlying Bharata Natyam is brought out most graphically and in a scientific manner in the very first complete dance sequence which a student of Bharata Natyam has to learn. This sequence is called the Alaripu. Prior to this, various stances and movements are taught. The Alaripu is the first *regular sequence* taught to the beginner. It is most significant in its purpose and its import, for in it we have the revelation of the Inner Sadhana of Bharata Natyam. I shall explain to you how this is so.

To understand the significance you must have an idea of the Alaripu. To state it simply, it is made up of rhythmic movements of all the various parts of the body, one after the other, in a definite order and sequence. These rhythmic movements are set to music and accurate and perfect timing. This timing of Talam is one of the most essential factors in the dance. The movements stated above range from movements of the eyebrows and end ultimately with movements with the soles of the feet. The hands and feet, of course, move most of the time in the performance of the dance. The dancer takes up the opening pose and commences the Nritya. This Nritya is usually done before the Deity. The dancer moves the eyebrows first. Secondly, movements are made with both the eyes and with beautiful rhythm the pupils of the eyes are made to dart from side to side and up and down. Next, in perfect rhythm again, the dancer moves the neck to the right and the left. This neck-movement is a most important item in the dance and is kept up throughout the dance. Forming the background of the whole sequence are an inspired smile and incessant movements of the neck and the eyes, the combined total effect of all the three being to indicate that the dedication of the soul is aimed cheerfully and spontaneously and that the result of the dedication is supreme and perfect happiness.

Now, the head movements over, the movements of hands follow. Starting with the shoulder, then the elbows and then the wrist, all these are deftly moved in beautiful well-controlled movements, which it is a real pleasure to watch and to follow. One of the features that enhances this beauty is the perfect symmetry with which both sides of the body, right as well as left, alternately execute these movements. The movement of the arms and hands are completed with a series of beautiful graduated motions of the open palms of the hand held in a definite scientific position. This over, the dancer next moves the chest, then the waist and then the hips. all in a graceful, well-defined manner and to accurate timing.

The graceful dance proceeds onward and the movements of the trunk now give place to those of the lower limbs. The thighs, the knees and the ankles are all skilfully brought into play and neat movements are deftly executed by the artist in the course of the dance. Movements of the feet follow, which ultimetely conclude with a thrilling finish with rapid manipulation of the soles and the dancer's feet upon the boards. This finale of pattering of the sole upon the floor is a sheer delight of wonderful rhythm and marvellous timing. Thus the Alaripu ends and the dance comes to a close with a beautiful prostration of Namaskar. From the physical point of view, this comprehensive dance movement is meant to serve as an excellent preparation for taking up the higher lessons. It prepares the dancer successfully by serving as an ideal, all-comprehensive exercise which enables the dancer to get control over every part of the body and to master the manipulations of them all with perfection, accuracy and grace.

Now you have in the Alaripu complete and comprehensive dance-movements of the entire body from the head right up to the soles of the feet. All the above-stated movements are done with utmost devotion and deep reverence. The entire dance is filled with fullest Bhav and the Bhav is that of earnest DEDICATION and COMPLETE SURRENDER. Herein is revealed the secret of the spiritual basis and the Inner Sadhana of Bharata Natyam. The movements of the entire body systematically, part by part, symbolises the dedication of your whole being in every aspect of its life here. Bharata Natyam will now be seen as an offering of oneself, an Arpana of one's entire being to the Divine Being. It is a spontaneous and exquisite sacrifice through art, at the altar of the Universal Being. Bharata Natyam is now seen to be the process of ecstatic and blissful Atma-nivedan. Deep sincerity and intense Bhav are the predominant elements in this process of Atma-nivedan. Bharata Natyam reveals through the Alaripu its aim and purpose, its meaning and significance. The Alaripu conveys to you the message "Oh! man, live a life of perfect dedication, live a life of complete surrender and sacrifice, let all parts of your being, let your entire life and all its activities, be offered most reverentially unto the Lord. Live for God. This is the way to come face to face with and to realise the Supreme Being." Alaripu is an exposition through dance of:

"Kayena vacha manasendriyairva,
Budhyatmanava prakrite-swabhavat,
Karomi yad-yat sakalam parasmai
Narayanayeti samarpayami"

It reveals through dance the Inner Gita Sadhana of:

"Yat karoshi yadasnasi yat juhoshi dadasi yat,
Yat tapasyasi kounteya tat kurushwa madarpanam."

Whatever you do with any part of your being, it is all verily worship of the Lord and is devotionally offered up unto Him in whole-souled dedication. This Bhav of surrender and dedication is the Philosopher's-stone, as it were, which transforms the base metal of mundane secular life into pure gold of spiritual Sadhana. The Bharata Natyam brings this message to you and the Alaripu reveals beautifully and graphically this process of full dedication of the entire being before the Lord.

ALARIPU

Ta dam ti ta ku di ku, ta ku ti ku ta di ki na thom

Taa thai thai ki ta tha ka tat tam tai kitataka

tam dhittham ki ta tha ka thai tat thai

tam dhittham ki ta tha ka thai tat thai

dhittham ki ta tha ka thai tat thai, ki ta tha ka tham

dhittham ki ta tha ka thai tat thai

tam dhittham thai tat thai, tam dhittham thai tat thai,

tam dhittham thai tat thai, tam dhittham thai tat tadai,

thai tadai, tam dhita thai tadai, tam dhita thai tadai,

tam dhita thai tadai, tam dhita tai tam dhita tai tadai.

tam dhittham ki ta tha ka thai dat thai, ki ta tha ka tham

dhit tham ki ta tha ka thai dat thai

tam dhittham thai tat thai, tam dhittham thai tat thai,

tam dhittham thai tat thai, tam dhittham thai tat thai,

tam dhittham thai tat thai, tam dhittham thai tatthai,

tam dhita thai tatthai, tam dhita thai tatthai,

tam dhita thai tatthai, tam dhita thai tatthai,

tam dhita thai tatthai, tam dhita thai tatai

tam dhita thai tahthai, tam dhita thai tathai,

tam dhita thai tathai, tam dhita thai tathai,

tam dhita thai tathai, tam dhita thai tathai.

tam dhittham ki ta tha ka thai tatthai ki ta tha ka tam

dhittham ki ta tha ka thai tatthai ki ta tha ka tam dhittham

ki ta tha ka thai tatthai ki ta tha ka tam dittham ki ta

(74)

tha ka thai tatthai ki ta tha ka tam dittham thai tatthai

tam dhittham thai tatthai, tam dhittham thai tatthai

tam dhita thai tathai, tam dhita thai tathai,

tam dhita thai tathai, tat dhita thai tatthai,

tam dhita thai tathai, tam dhita thai tathai,

tam dhita thai tathai, tam dhita thai tathai,

tam dhita thai tathai, tam dhita thai tathai,

tam dhita thai tathai, tam dhita thai tathai,

ta da ti tha ku ti ku di ku ta ku ta dhi ki na thom

di ki du tha ku di ki du tha ku di ki du tha ku

di ki du tha ku di ki du tha ku di ki du tha ku

di ki du tha ku di ki du tha ku di ki du tha ku

di ki du tha ku di ki du tha ku di ki du tha ku

ta dam ti ta ku di ku ta di ki na thom ta thai thai tam dhittham

LIVES OF NADA YOGIS

THYAGARAJA

Thyagaraja Swami was a great musician saint of South India. He was the father of South Indian music. He was a devotee of Lord Rama. Most of his devotional songs are in praise of Lord Rama. They are highly inspiring and soul-elevating.

Thyagaraja Swami is said to have composed 24,000 Kirtans (songs) in praise of Lord Rama. About five hundred songs only are sung by the songsters of the present day. When devotional songs are sung with piety and devotion, they at once elevate the soul to the magnanimous spiritual heights and melt the mind in the Lord and lead to communion and Bhava Samadhi.

Thyagaraja used to sing in the temple of Ambal at Trivadi and worship the Devi before he proceeded for his daily Bhiksha. He adopted the *unchha vritti* profession and lived on Bhiksha though he was well known throughout South India and many Maharajas were willing to have him as the Durbar songster.

Thyagaraja Swami was a superman. He had direct Darshan of Lord Rama on several occasions.

The then Raja of Pudukottah once tested the merits of the songsters in a strange way. He placed an unlit lamp amongst them. He challenged the experts to light the lamp with a song only, without using a match-stick or any other means. Thyagaraja Swami meditated upon Narada for a while, sung the Raga *"Jyotiswarupini"* and the lamp lighted of itself. All were struck with wonder.

Thyagaraja Swami restored to life a person who was accidentally drowned in a temple well, while he was returning from a pilgrimage to Tirupati. He had the knowledge of the correct day and hour of the passing away of his soul from the physical body. Divine Rishi Narada gave him the book named *"Swararnavam"* for propagating high-class music.

His Samadhi is at Thiruvaiyar (Trivadi) on the banks of the Cauveri, about seven miles from the town of Tanjore. All the songsters of South India assemble there and celebrate his anniversary with great éclat every year in the month of January.

Glory to Thyagaraja Swami whose songs instil devotion, joy and happiness in the hearts of hearers.

PURANDARA DAS

Purandara Das was a great poet and saint of Karnatak. He is a saint who belongs to the whole of India. He stands on a par with the great saints of other provinces, like Kabir, Surdas, Gauranga, Tukaram, Thyagaraja. Purandara Das was a great musician as well. He heard the music of the soul inside and so he gave his thrilling music outside.

Purandara Das lived during the glorious days of the Carnatic Empire of Vijayanagar in the sixteenth century. What Gauranga is to Bengal, Tukaram to Maharashtra, Mirabai to Marwar, Tulsi Das to United Provinces, Thyagaraja to Madras Presidency, Purandara Das is to Karnatic country.

Purandara Das was born in a rich, Brahmin family in 1484 A.D. at Purandharagarh, a town about fifteen miles from the modern city of Poona. Gauranga, Vallabhacharya and Purandhar Das ware contemporaries. Purandara Das worshipped Lord Vittala (Lord Krishna) the presiding deity in the famous pilgrimage centre of Pandharpur in Maharashtra.

Purandara Das is regarded as an Avatar of Narada Rishi. He is considered as the father of Carnatic system of music. He had profound knowledge of Raga and Tala. His contributions to Carnatic Sahitya are indeed very great. His literary style is exquisite.

He combined in himself command of language, beauty of expression, poetic genius, vast learning and scholarship of ancient writings in Sanskrit and sound knowledge of music in all its branches, harmony, rhythm, Natya or rhythmic movements with expressive Bhavas and also Aparokshanubhuti or realisation of Self.

Purandara Das initiated a line of saints which for centuries has spread throughout Karnataka the spiritual message. Krishnaraja was a disciple of Mahipathi who comes at the end of the line initiated by Purandara Das.

He spent forty years in the dissemination of Bhakti all over the land through his songs. He died at the age of 80 at Vijayanagar in 1564 A. D.

MIRA BAI

Mira is regarded as the incarnation of Radha. Mira Bai was brought up amidst *Vaishnava* influence, which moulded her life in the path of devotion towards Lord Krishna. She learnt to worship Sri Krishna from her childhood. When she was four years of age, she manifested religious tendencies. Once, there was a marriage-procession in front of her residence. The bridegroom was nicely dressed. Mira, who was only a child, saw the bridegroom and said to her mother innocently, "Dear mother, who is my bridegroom?" Mira's mother smiled and, half in jest and half in earnest, pointed towards the image of Sri Krishna and said, "My dear Mira, Lord Krishna—this beautiful image—is your bridegroom."

Child Mira began to love the idol of Krishna very much. She spent much of her time in bathing and dressing the image. She worshipped the image. She slept with the image. She danced about the image in ecstasy. She sang beautiful songs in front of the image. She used to talk with the idol.

Mira's father arranged for her marriage with Rana Kumbha of Chittore, in Mewar. She was a very dutiful wife. She obeyed her husband's commands implicitly. After her household duties were over, she would go to the temple of Lord Krishna, worship, sing and dance, before the image daily The little image would get up, embrace Mira, play on flute and talk to her.

Mira's fame spread far and wide. So many princes and queens have come and gone. So many Ranis, Kumaris, and Maharanis have appeared on the stage of this world and vanished. How is it that the queen of Chittore alone is still remembered? Is this on account of her beauty? Is this on account of her poetic skill? No, it is on account of her renunciation, one-pointed devotion to Lord Krishna and God-realisation. She came face to face with Krishna. She talked with Kirshna—her beloved. She drank the Krishna Prema Rasa. She has sung from the core of her heart the music of her soul, the music of her beloved, her unique spiritual experiences, and the songs of surrender and Prem.

She had the beautiful cosmic vision. She saw Krishna in the tree, in the stone, in the creeper, in the flower, in the bird, in all beings,—in everything. So long as there is the Name of Krishna, there will be the name of Mira also.

Her earthly life was full of troubles and difficulties. She was persecuted. She was tormented and yet she kept up an undaunted spirit and a balanced mind all through, by the strength of her devotion and grace of her beloved Krishna. Though she was a princess, she begged alms and lived sometimes on water alone. She led a life of perfect renunciation and self-surrender.

She had *Raganuga or Ragatmika Bhakti*. She did no ritualistic worship. She had spontaneous love for Lord Krishna. She did not practise Sadhana-Bhakti. From her very childhood she poured forth her love on Lord Krishna. Krishna was her husband, father, mother, friend, relative and Guru. Krishna was her Prananatha. She had finished the preliminary modes of worship in her previous birth.

She was fearless in her nature, simple in her habits, joyous in her disposition, amiable in her deportment, graceful in her behaviour and elegant in her demeanour. She immersed herself in love of *Giridhar Gopal*. The name of *Giridhar Gopal* was always on her lips. Even in her dreams, she lived and had her being in Sri Krishna.

In her divine intoxication she danced in public places. She had no sex-idea. Her exalted state could not be adequately described in words. She was sunk in the ocean of Prem. She had no consciousness of her body and surroundings. Who can guage the depth of her devotion? Who can understand her internal Premamaya state of Maha Bhava? Who can measure the capacity of her large heart? She wafted the fragrance of devotion far and wide. Those who came in contact with her, were affected by her strong current of Prem. She was like Lord Gauranga. She was an embodiment of love and innocence. Her heart was the temple of devotion. Her face was the lotus-flower of Prem. There was kindness in her look, love in her talk, joy in her discourses, power in her speech and fervour in her songs. What a marvellous lady! What a wonderful personality! What a charming figure!

Her mystic songs act as a soothing balm to the wounded hearts and tired nerves of those who turmoil in this world with the heavy burden of life. The sweet music of her songs exerts a benign influence on the hearers, removes discord and disharmony and lulls them to sleep. Her language of love is so powerful that even a downright atheist will be moved by her devotional songs.

Mira's songs infuse faith, courage, devotion and love of God in the minds of the readers. They inspire the aspirants to the path of devotion and produce in them a marvellous thrill, and melting of the heart.

Mira was the greatest of lady-saints who had the Realisation of the Supreme Beloved through divine dance and Sangeeta.

NADA JYOTI

Muthuswami Dikshitar

Muthuswami Dikshitar was born in the year 1775 at Tiruvarur in South India. His parents Sri Ramaswami Dikshitar and Srimati Subbulakshmi had done Anushthana at Vaitheeswaran Koil, as they had not been blessed with an offspring. One night Lord Muthukumaraswami appeared in Sri Ramaswami Dikshitar's dream and presented him with a garland of pearls (*Muthu*—in Tamil). Soon after this a son was born to them and they named him Muthuswami.

Muthuswami was full of spiritual Samskaras. Ever in his boyhood, he had the blessed good fortune of serving Yogis and sages. His father's Guru, Sri Chidambaranatha Yogi, noticing the boy's innate spirituality, took him to Banaras, where the Yogi initiated Muthuswami into the Guru-Mantra, and in the mysteries of higher music. The Yogi asked Dikshitar to return home; but the latter was reluctant. How was he to know that his Anushthana had borne fruit? The Yogi said: 'When you offer Arghya in the Ganga today, you will see in the water, whatever you wish for." Muthuswami thought of the Veena (the instrument in handling which he shone as a Master) and offered the Arghya. In the water, he saw a new resplendent, divine Veena. Even after this positive proof of his Siddhi, he was unwilling to leave the Guru . . . till shortly afterwards the Guru Himself left the mortal coil.

After receiving his father's blessings, Muthuswami left for Tiruttani to worship Lord Subramania there. As he was ascending the hill, an old man appeared before him and asked him to open his mouth. When he did so, the old man dropped a piece of sugarcandy in his mouth and disappeared. At that very instant, Dikshitar had Darshan of Lord Subramania. From that day Dikshitar began to regard Lord Subramania Himself as his Supreme Guru, and therefore all his compositions bear the Mudra "*Guru-Guha*".

Dikshitar has visited all the sacred shrines of South India; and he has sung inspiring songs in praise of all the Deities. That shows his deep Advaitic realisation and his profound devotion. His Navagraha Kirtans are famous and possess such a mysterious power that Dikshitar's own disciple Sri Tambiappan was cured of his chronic stomach-ache when he sang the Navagraha Kirtans. His Navarana Kirtans are repeated to bestow all the Divine Aiswaryas on the Nada Yogi who devoutly sings them.

With all this, Dikshitar remained poor in material wealth. Such is the glorious Lila of the Lord that He chooses to keep His Devotees in poverty and therefore away from the temptations of this earthly existence; and through their attitude to life and material wealth to place before other devotees the heart of a Para-Bhakta who wants God and nothing else and who, for the sake of God, is ready to endure any suffering and any privation. Dikshitar was approached by some of his friends who induced him to sing songs in praise of the Maharaja of Tanjore, to earn his favour and thereby wealth. Dikshitar refused: "I wouldn't sing in praise of this Bhogaraja or Bhojaraja. I will continue to sing songs in praise of Thyagaraja." When he had no money to pay taxes on his ancestral property, he gave it away to a poor Brahmin! When he had no food to eat, his wife became anxious. But Dikshitar went on singing the Lord's glories. Mysteriously a cartload of provisions were delivered at his house: a big officer due to arrive that day had not come—and so the provisions purchased for his sake were transferred to Dikshitar! Seeing this miracle. Dikshitar's wife began to entertain a desire: "Why should not my husband sing His Names and ask for golden ornaments for me?" The Lord understood her heart. That night she had a dream in which Goddess Lakshmi appeared to her bedecked in a great variety of divine ornaments: "Will this much do for you?" She asked. Dikshitar's wife was ashamed and enlightened. She got up and prostrated to Dikshatar and confessed her foolishness in desiring ornaments and after relating her experience assured him that she would never thereafter entertain a desire for ornaments.

Once he went to Kivalur to have Darshan of Akshayalinga. Pujari of the Temple had just closed the door of the Temple and refused to re-open it. Dikshitar sang his beautiful song: *"Akshayalinga-Vibho"* and the temple-door opened of its own accord.

Dikshitar once went in search of his brother Baluswami and had to pass through the Ettaiyapuram State. The State had had no rains at all for a considerable time and famine threatened to break out. Hearing this Dikshitar sang a song *"Anandamrita Varshini"*; at once it began to rain. He continued to sing *"Varshaya Varshaya"* and the rain continued, till he sang *"Sthambaya, Sthambhaya"* when the rain stopped. At Ettaiyapuram one day, the state elephant became mad and was doing havoc. When no one was able to control it, Dikshitar blessed a pinch of sacred ash and sent it; with it they were able to control the elephant, and it became normal again. Such is the wonderful power of the prayers of a man-of-God, which he occasionally uses, not for his own sake, not for the sake of gaining any selfish ends, but for the sake of mankind, for relieving human misery.

In the year 1835, on the Dipavali day, Sri Baluswami was singing some of Dikshitar's Kritis when, with the utterance of the Names of Devi, Dikshitar cast off his mortal coil and attained the Supreme Seat of Nada-Brahma.

Glory, Glory to the Immortal Muthuswami Dikshitar, the great Nada Jyoti!

SYAMA SASTRIGAL

Syama Sastrigal was born in 1763 at Tiruvarur in South India. He was a born-musician. He enjoyed the abundant grace of Mother Kamakshi; he was born in a family of Goddess Kamakshi's worshippers.

He learnt the rudiments of music from his own uncle. But no one in the family was really proficient in music. That was his only, though great, obstacle. Unlike Sri Thyagaraja and Sri Dikshitar, Syama Sastrigal never knew poverty. His family was always in affluent circumstances. His own dress and demeanour bore witness to this; but at heart he was humility incarnate.

His music did not find favour with his uncle and his father. They were against his singing. But the gifted boy could not restrain his natural talent. God's Grace came in the form of a Sadhu, Sangitaswami of Kashi. When this Sadhu visited Syama Sastrigal's house, he told Syama's father that the boy was bound to shine as one of the greatest musicians of the day and that he should therefore be given all facilities to learn music. This made the family yield; and they let the boy learn Sangita from the Sadhu himself, who was then staying at Tanjore for the Chaturmasya. Within those four months, Syama Sastrigal had attained a rare mastery of the art and science of music. At the conclusion of the Chaturmasya, the Guru blessed Syama Sastrigal and departed.

Syama Sastrigal was a great Devotee of Devi. Through Her Grace, he had acquired Vak-Siddhi also. Whatever he said came true. He knew Mantra-Sastra and Jyotisha also. He was able to give predictions by merely looking at a person!

In those days there was another musician called Bobbili Kesaviah who prided himself in his knowledge of music. He used to go about challenging other musicians and defeating them. He came to Tanjore—the greatest seat of music then—as he thought that if he defeated the best of musicians there, he would undoubtedly be regarded as the supreme monarch of the music-world. The Maharaja of Tanjore requested Syama Sastrigal to meet Kesaviah. Though normally Sastrigal would not attend the Court, he went in order to uphold the honour of Tanjore and to quell Kesaviah's pride. Kesaviah was easily defeated by the divine child of Kamakshi. Who can stand before the Lord's Grace?

Similarly on another occasion, Syama Sastrigal defeated another arrogant musician—Appu Kutty.

Syama Sastrigal passed away in 1827 singing the glory of Mother Kamakshi and meditating upon Her.

His compositions—and there were 300 of them—are very rich in melody and in literary quality.

VEENA DHANAM

It is often said that the aim of all instrumental music should be to approximate to, if not imitate, that of the human voice. This idea has gained   musicians who did justice to it. They are the Siddha Vidhyadhari and the late Simili Sundarm Ayyar, one of Thomas Gray's "Full many a gem of purest ray serene." Thanks to the persuasive endeavour of the late C. R. Srinivasa Ayyangar, Dhanammal recorded the Begada Varnam in 1936, on a gramophone disc. Suffice it to say that it is a Roman Colosseum for those who can perceive its majestic architecture.

Lastly, a word about the Kriti and similar types of composition set to definite time-measures or *Talam*. How many of us are aware of the bedrock of Carnatic Music, viz., the twenty-two Srutis? If our music has to come to its own and deliver its message to the world, we have to rebuild the crumbling edifice from its very foundation. It is a vexed problem and needs a Hercules to tackle it. Again, it was given only to the two solitary figures mentioned above to hold fast to the banner. For those who care, a few records of Dhanammal, which still linger in odd corners here and there provide the clue to this secret of Carnatic Music.

SRIMATI RUKMINI DEVI

Srimati Rukmini Devi, the founder-President of the world-renowned Kalakshetra, the International Arts Centre, Madras, was born in the gracious year of 1904. Of the contemporary world, she is the backbone of Bharata Natyam. It is appropriate to say, she is the divine dance incarnate. Every individual genius is incomparable and unique; more so, Srimati Rukmini Devi, who has breathed vigorous life into the much neglected and almost dying art of Bharata Natyam.

The illustrious daughter of Pandit Sri Nilakanta Sastri, played her way into the most worthy and rich lap of Dr. Annie Besant, the Western Star in the spiritual firmament of the East, and gradually unfolded her heaven-born genius and god-given talents. This never-fading lily bloomed under the sunshine of Dr. Besant. Intrinsic excellence has found its fullest expression in her.

In the year 1920 she was married to a great soul, Dr. G. S. Arundale, who was the President of the Theosophical Society from 1934 to 1945. The Arundale Montessori Training Centre for teachers, at Adayar, Madras, was founded by her. She is versatile and her activities are multifarious. She is Adhyaksha of the Dr. V. Swaminatha Iyer Tamil Library, the Vice-President of Indian Humanitarian League, the President of the World Federation of the Young Theosophists, and the Director of Besant Theosophical School. The Editor of "The Young Citizen", Srimati Rukmini Devi weilds an inspiring pen; her subjects range from Education and Art to Theosophy and Religion. She has a fascinating way of speaking; her speech is fluent; her accent is clear. The true representative of the sublimest arts, the art of Bharata Natyam, is quite humble, extremely noble and saintly.

Srimati Rukmini Devi has made deep researches in dance, music and drama. "The Light of Asia", "Incidents from the Life of Bhishma", "Karaikal Ammayar" (Tamil), "Rukmini Swayamvaram"(Kathakali), "Kutrala Kuravanji" (Temple drama), are among her many brilliant dramatic productions. Her superb dance recitals and lectures given all over India and abroad, are too well known to need any mention. Her art is sacred to her heart. It is her mode of divine worship. To any critical eye, it is clear, that the Grace of the Supreme Dancer Lord Siva, of the Charming Krishna, of the ever-singing Narada, has descended upon her abundantly.

Today when the world is thick with the stifling smoke of Sybaritism, profiligate dance and revelries, she is the chaste Figure come into this world, standing for complete Purity in Dance, and for Dance as the most important and effective method of seeking communion with the Lord in whom we live, move and have our being.

SRI R. RANGARAMANUJA IYENGAR

नौमि सरस्वतीं देवीं तत्स्वरूपां धनं तथा ।

रङ्गरामानुजार्यं च पद्मां च तत्पदाश्रिताम् ॥

Sri R. Rangaramanuja Iyengar is a glorious repository of the Nada-Yoga-Mahavidya that had incarnated in Veena Dhanammal, one of the greatest Nada-Yoginis of recent memory. She has done to Carnatic Music what the great Avataras of the Lord and the saints of Bharatavarsha have done to Dharma. It was perhaps she and she alone who restored Carnatic Music to its rightful place as a Sadhana, as Yoga, by shifting the emphasis from vocal gymnastics to Bhava-Yukta Sangeeta. This the old muse bequeathed to Sri Iyengar, a true disiciple of Veena Dhanammal.

Sri Rangaramanuja Iyengar hails from the Tanjore District in South India, the Janma-Bhumi of the Holy Trinity of the Music World—Sri Thyagaraja, Sri Muthuswami Dikshitar and Sri Shyama Sastrigal. Mannargudy—Sri Iyengar's own family, in particular—was a garden in which the fragrant (though 'silent') flowers of pure music continually blossomed forth. If hereditary instincts bore fruit, it was very much so in Sri Iyengar's case. Though not a musical technician, his father, Sri Raghunathaswami Iyengar had a sensitive "ear" for music and this sensitivity worked itself out to a fuller bloom in his offspring.

Sri Rangaramanuja Iyengar evinced a passionate interest in and exquisite taste for music even as a boy of eight or ten. Such was his innate capacity to make a mental record of the music that he listened to and to reproduce it at will, that he was much sought after by great connoisseurs of those days for a faithful reproduction of musical concerts in and around Mannargudy in Tanjore district.

He never rested on his oars. In his relentless pursuit after good music, Sri Iyengar courted all kinds of hardships. He would foot great distances to master the various techniques wherever they were available. Differences in caste or social status never mattered to him at all. The quest for Sad-Vidya alone spurred him on, till he was ready for the Message of Nada Yoga that Veena Dhanammal had for him.

Sri Rangaramanuja Iyengar came into contact with Veena Dhanammal in 1926. Ever since, it has been a case of unquestioning surrender to that Grand Muse. The way he absorbed the technique was a marvel in itself. Dhanammal's music was as elusive as it was divine. And Sri Iyengar was so greatly awed by its subtle nuances that often he wondered if it was possible for a mere human being to rise to such dizzy heights. Yet, the desire to imbibe was too great to resist. Hence, Fridays invariably found the ardent music-lover at the feet of the Muse, silently observing the tender fingers of the old woman as they danced on the divine instrument, producing celestial music. His inborn powers of reducing the music to notation added greatly to his stature as an admirably receptive student.

Strangely enough, the Guru was not for long aware of a student in Sri Iyengar! Almost with Ekalavya's devotion, Iyengar carried on his mission with different phases of hope, despair and indefatigable industry. A radio concert in 1936—after ten years of unostentatious discipleship—brought Iyenqar into the good graces of Dhanammal; she was most agreeably surprised when she heard, through a receiving set, Sri Iyengar's Veena recital, broadcasting music that was characteristically her own! Time and again the glorious Muse would recount with profound admiration and regard, her reaction to Sri Iyengar's maiden performance. Needless to say, the inevitable result of this was Sri Iyengar's initiation, as it were, by Sri Veena Dhanammal into the mysteries of higher music. Today Sri Iyengar shines as a worthy—if not the only—and true disciple of Dhanammal, and leads a life dedicated to the propagation of the celestial music that had taken refuge in Sri Dhanammal.

A unique feature about him is that he has a very high level of general education—he is a B.A., L.T.—sustained by regular habits of reading. This rare combination of musical and literary attainments has guarded him against the parochialisms of the traditional "Bhagavatars" who very often prove fossilised entities. He goes about with an open mind ready to grasp novelties as they come to him. His is a synthetical mind. His vocation as a schoolmaster is a further blessing. It gives him a sure insight into the students' difficulties and need, and hence, too, his method of teaching makes an interesting study.

Sri Iyengar maintains an uncompromising standard of perfection. Nothing satisfies him, that falls short of true Nada Yoga, which promotes finer impulses by its moving quality. To him, as to his preceptor, music is a vehicle for higher (spiritual) pursuits and not a commodity for lesser ends: this he actually demonstrated during his Malayan tour when, at the request of a foreign Yoga student Sri Iyengar played some special melodies on the Veena and the Yoga student later disclosed that as he sat there listening to the music, his consciousness was lifted up to great heights. Sri Iyengar is firm in his conviction that pure music forms part of Yoga Sadhana and awakens Kundalini Sakti, and, therefore, should not be made to subserve the baser instincts of man, by making it sensuous. This explains why he has fought shy of the limelight all along.

This great Nada Yogi of our times has rendered yeoman service to the cause of music in quite a number of ways. His masterly publications entitle him to the gratitude of posterity. In 1934 he startled the music-world by editing "Keertanamalai" for Brahma-Sri Papanasam Sivan, an inspired composer of the South. In 1941 again he gave to music lovers a compilation of 75 of Purandaradasa's pieces entitled "Purandaramanimalai"— the first of its kind. These early efforts were but the spring boards for greater achievements to come.

The year 1947 saw the 100th anniversary of Saint Thyagaraja. Conferences were convened and resolutions were passed that the great saint's composition—or whatever was available of his 24,000 Kritis —should be unearthed, edited and published. These pious resolutions however, were still born. Moved by an exalted idealism, Sri Iyengar embarked on this great venture. The first volume of 'Kritimanimalai' stirred the music world. There was rousing reception at the hands of music lovers and devotees of Thyagaraja. Soon the project swelled into a series of six volumes. The Press and the public hailed the endeavour as the pioneer work in the field of music. No praise can be too high for such an achievement. The six Volumes of the Kritimanimalai are a standing monument to Sri Iyengar's invincible self-confidence, unyielding tenacity of purpose, untiring industry, supreme mastery of his subject and his unbounded love for it.

Yet another way in which he seeks to disseminate Dhanammal's message is by conducting cultural tours in India and abroad. In 1951 Sri Iyengar was invited to Malaya and Singapore for delivering demonstrational lectures on Indian music. It was a phenomenal success. Iyengar has travelled all over India, and addressed several gatherings, besides giving Veena recitals.

Sri Iyengar has also been training students, without a mercenary motive. Mr. Harold S. Powers, a full-bright scholar from the U.S.A., was under Sri Iyengar for 2 years, when the intelligence of the teacher and the taught worked together admirably towards making a regular musician of Mr. Powers. The public performances that the latter gave at the U.S.I.S., Madras, and under the auspices of the International Fellowship were eloquent tributes to the extraordinary teaching ability of Sri Iyengar. Sri Iyengar is an engaging conversationalist and during the course of a casual conversation, abounding in anecdotes of his and Dhanammal's life, he would instill into the listener his sublime tenets concerning music. He would inspire the student to aspire for the highest in music and not be carried away by theoretical discussions, for, he would declare, Music, like everything divine, is beyond the intellect and is not confined to codes and conventions though they might be necessary as guide-posts.

The foremost among his students is perhaps his own daughter Sri R. Padma, M.A., who has had the rarest good fortune of commencing her education in music at the early age of 5. Today she not only shines as a replica of her father but as the very embodiment of Sri Dhanammal's music. Guided by her father, her own intuition has led her to region where till then only Dhanammal had access. Padma broadcasts frequently from the Madras A.I.R., and joins her father in concerts. She has been accompanying Sri Iyengar on all his tours at home and abroad. Those who have heard her confirm that her music is a faithful echo of Dhanammal's.

Such is his ardent desire to spread Dhanammal's music, Sri Iyengar is ready to travel to the ends of the earth to teach this Nada Yoga Mahavidya. Recently he came all the way from Madras to Rishikesh, to teach Veena to Sri Swami Venkatesanandaji (a disciple of Sri Swami Sivananda Ji Maharaj) who has had the rare blessing of having Sri Iyengar for his Veena-Guru. The ready response on the part of student gives Iyengar a chance to serve —and that has been his mission all along.

SIVANANDA'S VOICE—THE VOICE OF GOD

(Sri Swami Sivananda-Hridayananda)

Swamiji's voice, Ah! what an enchanting, wonderful voice it is! It is indeed the voice of God, a voice that directly speaks to the soul, a voice of inspiration, joy, peace, strength, purity, love and power. No one who has heard it once can forget it again. It will ring and linger in the ears for ever with its sacred sweetness.

Mind is always attracted by sweet sounds. Even the cobra is enchanted by sweet music.

A voice super-charged with divine power is one of the most powerful contrivance by which the mind can be made to withdraw from other external influences and forced to rest in one-pointed attention and absorption.

The sound vibrations have unlimited power. Instances have been quoted to show that the power of sound vibrations by itself can light lamps, produce or stop rain, etc. Sound has also got the power of curing diseases and relaxing nervous tension.

Swami Sivanandaji's voice is the voice of the Universal Eternal Heart, and hence it releases spiritual forces that set into vibration every individual heart. It is a voice unspeakably rich with subtle emotions of divine love and sweetness and rings with the rapture of Self-realisation. Just like the musical vibrations of the flute of Lord Krishna, it penetrates the soul of his devotees. The thrilling richness of his tone, the grace and ease with which it can be raised to any pitch and the appropriate proportion of its volume, combined with its unbounded spiritual power, makes it the most perfect and wonderful voice in the world. It awakens reverence and divine love, and as if by the

(99)

touch of a magic wand floods the whole being with peace and bliss.

His kind and loving words touch the very core of one's being and dispel the darkness of ignorance and fill the heart with the light of divine aspiration. Swamiji speaks gently, sweetly, soothingly, truthfully and speaks only what is good—in measured words. His voice is one of the most effective means by which he is able to elevate the minds of human beings to sublime heights of divine splendour.

When Swamiji addresses a bigger audience, his voice becomes very powerful. It can be heard at a long distance without the aid of a loudspeaker. Words of wisdom pour out from him with divine authority mingled with humility. His appealing and inspiring words tear the veil of worldliness by which men are enveloped and expand their soul. People stand spellbound by the effect of his magnetic orations. The divine messages conveyed through his soul-penetrating voice leave a lasting impression on the listeners and transform even the confirmed atheists into devout theists.

It is a very rare treat to the ears to hear Swamiji chant the sacred monosyllable "OM." The sound 'OM' is the first manifestation of the Absolute, and hence it is not a wonder that one experiences an inner harmony and feels the nearness of God when Swamiji, the God in human form, starts chanting 'OM' with feeling and Bhav. The powerful vibrations of his voice impregnated with the dynamic force of godliness floats over the space, filling it with sanctity, and invisible fingers pull at the heart-strings of the listeners inspiring them with overwhelming devotion. There is something in his voice that seems to set up a connecting link between heaven and earth, something that makes one feel that one is wafting in a strange space of beauties and joys, far away from this world, but nearest to God. This wonderwoking voice in a mysterious way, manages to force open the inner chamber of the heart and turns and controls the mind.

Swamiji's music is a rare blending of rhythm, metre and melody. It is nothing but an expression of his ecstatic communion with God. In the blissful joy of listening to his melodious voice, one forgets all the cares and distractions of this mundane existence and at least for the moment feels as though the soul has been released from its human prison to enjoy the company of its Eternal Beloved. The nectar of his delightful music acts as an intoxicating drink and drowns one in divine madness.

To help those who have no patience to listen to lengthy religious discourses, he makes use of his singing capacity to enlighten them. His songs contain the essence of spiritual Sadhana, philosophy, Vedanta and Bhakti, etc., and he sings them in different languages.

Thus through the medium of his omnipotent-voice, the divine vibrations of the Eternal Spirit, Swamiji continues to disseminate spiritual knowledge to each and every one who comes to him.

I pray to God to give my beloved Gurudev, best of health, long life and powerful voice, so that he may lead us safely across the ocean of life.

THE MAHARSHI'S MUSIC

(Sri Swami Sivananda)

1. I am Alpha-Omega

I am the beginning

I am the end

I am Alpha and Omega

I am the light of lights

I am pure consciousness

I am everfree

I am Eternity, Infinity

I am Immortal Bliss

I am that I am

2. I Lost and Gained

I purified

I meditated

I lost my body

I lost my senses

I lost my mind

I lost my intellect

I lost my ' little I'

But I gained the All-full Brahman thereby

3. Bliss Consciousness am I

I am not the body

I am not the mind
I am not the ego
I am not the intellect
I am not the vital airs
Changeless am I
Formless am I
Omnipresent am I
The Eternal Witness am I
Bliss-Consciousness am I
Immortal and Eternal am I

4. Real Poverty

Lack of wealth is not poverty
Lack of virtue is real poverty
Lack of Knowledge of Atman is real poverty
Lack of discrimination is real poverty
Lack of dispassion is real poverty
Lack of Vichara is real poverty
Lack of serenity is real poverty
Lack of four means is real poverty
Lack of devotion is real poverty
Lack of Japa-treasure is real poverty

5. 1 DO NOT WANT ANY LIFE HERE

Fifty years are spent in sleep.
Out of remaining fifty
Fifteen years are spent in childhood

Some in disease
Some in old age
Some in quarrel, weeping etc.
There is no real enjoyment in this world
I do not want any life here
I want Immortal Bliss of Atma.

6. BAMBOO AND JIVA

Bamboo has four defects
It is very proud of its great height
It is hollow.
It has knots all over the body
It contains fire and consumes itself
The Jiva also is proud of his wealth, position, etc.
He is also hollow, no knowledge of Self
He has also Knots of Avidya, Kama, Karma
He is consumed by the fire of lust and anger.

7. ONE I SEE

One exists
One I see
One I serve
One I love
One I know
One I worship
One I adore
One I feel

8. WHERE ART THOU, BELOVED

I am sleepless,

I have heard the Voice of my Beloved,

I long to meet Him.

My eyes do ache

For a sight of my Beloved.

When, O when wilt Thou come, Beloved?

Where, O where

Art Thou, Beloved,

The King of my heart?

THIRD ANNIVERSARY OF SIVANANDA MUSIC COLLEGE

(Swami Chidanandaji's speech on 1.2.1956)

It is a happy coincidence that the anniversary of our Music College is also on the Thyagaraja Anniversary Day, because in setting up the Music College, Swami Sivanandaji has a twofold purpose, inasmuch as his work is to bring about an all-round regeneration of the culture of Bharatavarsha, though the prime importance and emphasis is given to the spiritual aspect of our culture, the Adhyatma Samskriti, yet he has made it his policy not to neglect the other and lesser aspects of the culture of Bharatavarsha. Naturally therefore, the aesthetics of this land also received their due share in doing this work of regeneration of Bharatiya-Samskriti and music being one of the salient features of the aesthetics of and country's culture, he is ever intent upon encouraging musicians, development of art in all possible ways. Therefore here Swamiji always gives a priority to the votaries of music. Swamiji encourages them in all ways, praises them, recommends them to others, gives them awards. He enthuses a man to pursue his avocation of music keenly and to enter into deeper practice of music.

Apart from bringing about a regeneration of the country's culture, the other factor is distinctive of his mission. That is in as much as music is a part and parcel of the Bhakti Yoga Sadhana where singing of Lord's praises and Bhajan is one of the indispensable Angas (Kirtan is an indispensable Anga of Navavidha Bhakti), in as much as music is a thing which refines emotion, develops the emotion of the devotee and gradually draws the mind inward, and is very conducive to the concentration of mind, so that by singing the Lord's Name,

(106)

one's mind gets more and more absorbed, the mind becomes slowly merged into the contemplation of the Ishta Devata, therefore music is a great help to all followers of the path of devotion, and so as a direct means of helping people upon the path of devotion and enabling them to refine their Bhav, and get better concentration and to help them on to emotional inwardness (ultimately it may take the devotee for Bhavasamadhi), music has been prescribed by Swamiji to all aspirants. Even if you are a Vedantin you must know how to sing Om, how to chant Om. How wonderful is the "Song of Chidananda" and the "Song of bliss"! Even if you are a Vedantin it will be of great help to you in attaining the Vedantic Bhav.

And music is something which gives life to all gatherings. Dry lecture,—it is only people with deep interest in the subject and people who have disciplined themselves to concentrate their mind upon anything which they wish to listen to, it is only to such people lectures can be of use, otherwise, after a few minutes the mind of the listeners will go elsewhere. Suppose some Bhajan is sung in the middle, a new life is created, and the wandering of the mind is arrested. Therefore, music has become a part and parcel of the Ananda Kutir Satsanga. So that this indispensable part and parcel may become more and more developed and improved in quality, a Music College has been started. It gives a wonderful opportunity for people to sit at the feet of the holy principal Swami Nadabrahmanandaji who is a man of high attainment in music, and specially God has endowed him with a special knack of teaching music and Kirtan in a wonderfully short period of time. Immediatly a person comes to the Ashram, he goes to office and sees Swamiji. Swamiji will ask him, "Are you going to stay?" "Yes." "Go to Nada Brahmanandaji and learn some Kirtan. You will have to sing tonight". When Swamiji leaves the office the person goes to Swami Nadabrahmanandaji and Nadabrahmanandaji teaches him two or three Kirtans. In the evening Satsanga Swamiji asks him, "Are you ready?" "Yes", and immediately a new Kiratan is sung. Swami Nadabrahmanandaji has got that wonderful knack of teaching people with surprising quickness and naturally people who have come into contact with Swami Nadabrahmanandaji have soon begun to sing new Kirtans. All these Bhajans have made a great stir. This year also we had been to Narendranagar, and all the listeners said, "Please see if you can record this music." They all wanted to learn music. In Roorkee he made a sensation and all those people who listened to his music became his disciples. They come and sit in the office until Gurudev returns to his Kutir, and after that they go to Swami Nadabrahmanandaji and learn Kirtans, and through his enthusiasm he has brought out a number of leaflets of choice Kirtans. They are invaluable to all Bhaktas. In addition to the music in them, they are Bhajans of prayer, and these songs if they are sung with meaning, they at once bring about a great transformation in the mind of the people. They infuse in us devotion. Therefore, for sublimating our emotion, Bhajan and music is of great help. It is in order to keep more and more people interested in this Sadhana that the Music College has been working and it has trained about three hundred students since its inception. Everyone who comes here becomes a student. Swami Nada Brahmanandaji is maintaining a register of all students who have learned new Bhajans. About three hundred people have been his students during this year since the college has been working.

It is only when you learn music and hear others singing beautiful music that you come to know what you have been missing by not having developed this art, and therefore, all can take advantage of this opportunity of tuition from the Music College. Many people have already learned many Ragas. All can study for fifteen minutes or half an hour if they can get time.

It is a way of refining their emotion and getting additional knowledge of music.

Thus this Music College will be a centre of Nada Yoga and Bhakti Yoga, and it will be a great help in bringing about quick progress in the Sadhana of all aspirants who are following Bhakti Yoga, and also it will be a powerful medium for propagating the ideals and teachings of Sri Gurudev, because a great deal of Gurudev's life-giving, soul-awakening Upadesh is put in the form of songs. The one book, "Inspiring Songs and Kirtans" is quite enough to give one all knowledge on Bhakti, Yoga and Vedanta. The songs in that book contain in a concentrated form the very essence of Bhakti, Gyana and Yoga, and these songs, have also been translated into Hindi in the Bhajanavali and if more and more people who are trained by Swami Nadabrahmananda take to learning these great Yoga-Vedantic lessons, then they can become wonderful propagators of the ideals of Divine Life. It will be much more effective than lecturing, because it will reach vaster and greater number. The masses should be awakened by this novel method of Yoga Sadhana. Therefore, let us pray that the Music College will grow from success to success and it may train a large number of devotees of Gurudev and all people who come in contact with Gurudev. Let us pray that the grace of God may soon make it a centre for the propagation of Divine Life ideals, and may this Music College ever be a centre of Nada Yoga, Bhakti Yoga and Karma Yoga of propagating the Divine Life ideals through Bhajans and Sankirtan all over the world.

THE SCIENCE OF THAAN

Swami Nadabrahmanandaji's Rare Mastery

(By Sri Swami Chidananda)

The term Thaan implies, to put it simply, a musical flourish executed vocally by a songster, rendered either in Sahitya form or through pure Alapana. It is usually made up of a chain of successive note patterns that are either made to culminate in a sudden climax, or made to synchronise to a marvel of most accurate timing or gracefully worked round into a circle, as it were, to a logical conclusion that could be anticipated to a nicety by the experienced hearer with a trained ear and musical maturity. Two points may be noted here, viz., that the Thaan is a medium employed solely by the vocalist, and secondly, in the process of weaving out the notational pattern, the singer does not pronounce the Swara or musical note, but just intones it. Each Thaan forms a unit by itself or rather, a unitary series of notes linked together to form a complete pattern. It is mostly executed with rapidity and is perfectly and accurately timed when in the course of a song (Geet) with its definite Taal. It may be observed that Thaan and its variants, *ulta-pulta,* are always executed only in the Chaupat or the higher 'Kaalaas' or tempo, and not in the first two lower tempos, or the Chauka and Madhyama Kaalaas, as they are known in the Dakshinadhi, or Southern schools. The mode employed for 'Visthara' (musical elaboration) in these two Kaalaas usually take the form of the Aalaap and the Gamak and Kathak. The first, viz., the Aalaap is in the Vilambit or Chauka Kaalaa. The second and third viz., Gamak and Kathak are in the Duppat, approximating to the Madhyama, also known.as the second Kaalaa.

The Science of Thaan had its greatest exponent in Thaan

Sen, the Master songster, who flourished in the heyday of the Moghul Empire under Akbar, the Great. Thaan Sen was Akbar's Court musician and a great favourite of the Emperor. He developed this intricate science to the highest peak of perfection. The countless Thaans that Thaan Sen created are claimed by his followers to number up to "Unnchas Koti Thaan," viz., forty-nine crores. Whatever the degree of validity of this claim, yet, it is undeniable that this gifted master who had attained the highest Siddhi in Sangeeta has left behind innumerable Thaans to posterity written down by him in voluminous manuscripts, some of which are said to be in the close custody of the line of musicians descendent from him. They style themselves as belonging to the "Thaan Sen Gharana." A great living exponent of this science of Thaan is Swami Nadabrahmananda.

Swami Nada Brahmanandaji has attained a rare mastery over this most difficult science by an extremely painstaking and arduous period of discipleship under masters of the Thaan Sen Gharana. Chiefly he attributes his knowledge to intense training under two masters, viz., for a period of three years under the venerable Alladiya Khan of Kolhapur State, and under the aged Tata Bua of Banaras for another period of seven years. These were years of unremitting toil, training, personal service and laborious practice. Nada Brahmanandaji practised day and night. He could hardly get enough sleep. He kept practising far into the small hours of the morning. He has now attained such a degree of mastery in this line that he shines as a unique phenomenon among exponents of today. He manifests an amazing control over the vocal system. Manipulating his articulation in most intricate manners to perfect and split second timings, he is able to produce Thaan of astonishing types that could be hardly thought capable of being produced.

The secret of Nada Brahmanandaji's genius may be said to

lie in his control over the rate of vibration and its location in any part of the body at will. By this technique it is claimed that various diseases affecting different parts of the body can be cured as well as prevented through this internal vibration. The impulse of vocal vibration is diverted along any limb or the trunk to any part of the anatomy even as a current of electricity is directed along the circuit to any desired place or object. The peculiar feature here is that the vocal vibration thus directed is of the same rate of the corresponding Thaan that is being produced by the singer at a particular moment. Swami Nada Brahmanandaji is himself a living testimony to this claim and he has not known a single day of illness.

The following are some of the Thaans from the repertoire of Sri Swami Nada Brahmanandaji:

Ratt Thaan: It is produced in the centre of the throat-region by a rapid vibration of the vocal chord, which are brought together in a short clapping movement within the throat. The sound thus produced is in the nature of a short, hacking note, giving a staccato effect. It clears out all phlegm. The practitioner becomes free from 'Kapha' Roga or diseases arising from the disbalance of the phlegmatic humour specially in its manifestation in the region of the chest and above it.

Gala-ka-Thaan: This is produced in the central region of the throat in the gullet portion in front of the neck and involves the manipulation of the Adam's Apple in a most extraordinary manner, setting it into an oscillatory motion of the utmost rapidity. Notes thus oscillated produce the strange effect of a chord of music echoing and re-echoing within the multiple arches of the ceiling of a Gothic Cathedral. Gala-ka-Thaan is a reliable weapon in the hands of the vocalist. It is a great desideratum of the voice culturist. From simple soar throat to congestive and inflammatory conditions of the larynx give way before the regular and systematic practice of this Thaan. Unlike the Ratt Thaan, there is comparatively lesser sacrifice of melody in the employment of this Thaan.

Aandolan Thaan: The location now is the actual mouth cavity. Aandolan is the vibrant notation produced with the help of the Uvula or the small tongue, which is set into motion at an incredible rate. Hence, the significant name Aandolan, which means swinging suspended as in fact the Uvula is. This Thaan cures all varieties of dry cough, arising out of local irritation of throat and palate and not caused by phlegm.. The exercise of the Aandolan Thaan gives rise to a novel and not unpleasant sound of somewhat restricted volume.

Ot Thaan: Thaan produced solely by manipulation of the lips or Ot. The volume of sound is still further restricted in the employment of this Thaan. It has a stimulating effect upon the entire frontal dental region of the incisors and bicuspids. Dental roots are toned up. Ensures mouth health in the practitioner.

Nasika Thaan: In this Thaan the vibration is located within the nasal passage just beneath the bridge. It provides a powerful shake-up to that region and acts as a vigorous cleanser and toner. It combats colds, coryza and rhinitis. It banishes adenoids. It is something in the nature of a 'netikriya,' without the use of thread or water; or in other words a 'Shabda-neti,' if one may employ such a term.

Bada jeeb-ka-Thaan: As the name denotes, this Thaan is produced with the help of the tongue itself being brought into vibratory motion. It is claimed that stuttering and stammering can be overcome through a regular practice of this Thaan.

Danta Thaan: In executing this Thaan, the dental thaan, the rapid side-to-side movement of lower row of teeth is employed to set the notes into vibration. The notes are articulated plain from the throat. They issue as plain notes without any sort of 'Gamak' or Tremelo until they reach the teeth and here, in their passage between the latter, the vibration is imparted by the singer. This Thaan also has the effect of strengthening the teeth.

Bina jeeb-ka-Thaan: Here the tongue is held tightly clenched between the teeth, with the tip projecting outside the lips. Thus, all movement of the tongue is completely arrested. In this position of fixity, the singer weaves out his Thaan with rapidity of execution and rate of vibration. The movement involves the root of the tongue.

Chhati-ka-Thaan: Here the voice is brought out powerfully right from the lungs with vigorous impulse imparted from the region of the chest. This is not uncommon among Gawais. One who practises Chhati-ka-thaan need have no fear of heart troubles.

Pet-ka-Thaan: This is a powerful exercise by which the practitioner thoroughly shakes up the entire gastrointestinal system. This Thaan depends for its vibration upon the forceful movement of the diaphragm as well as the entire stomach wall. The rectus abdominal muscles are brought into vigorous play during this Thaan. No person however strong can succeed in arresting the movement of the singer's stomach despite whatever pressure he may exert upon it. All the abdominal viscera are invigorated and toned up by the Pet-ka-thaan.

Threefold practice of Tara, Madhyama and Nabhi: Now we have a process to perfect which is the ardent ambition of almost all vocal masters. It is a production of sound in three pitches. In the Tara Swara, Swami Nada Brahmananda locates the voice vibrations in a most inexplicable manner upon the top of his head. He does this in a mysterious manner and when this Tara Thaan is in progress, a person placing his hand on the top of the singer's head will be startled to find the skull beneath his hand communicating the thrilling vibration corresponding to the Thaan in progress at the particular moment.

For the Madhya, the vibration is located in the central

point at the base of the throat between the two collar bones about the region where they join the sternum. Whatever Thaan the singer produces with his voice held in this state of Madhya is felt only at this point.

From here the singer suddenly drops down, as it were, and seems to reach into the very root point of articulate sound. The voice, is now seen to issue from deep down out of the region of the Nabhi or the navel. Holding on to this Nabhi Swara, we see him execute again with the same mastery all the intricacy of Thaan, *ulta-pulta*, both in 'bol' as well as in the 'khat' form.

The above practice of Thaan in this threefold Tara, Madhya and Nabhi, Nada is done with a degree of facility, with the singer switching abruptly from one pitch to another with such perfect ease and control, that is at once admirable and astounding. This difficult Triple Sadhana has mysterious effects and benefits the entire system of the practitioner. The breath vibrations help to awaken various hidden forces in the body, give abundant resistance power against diseases and grant a peculiar immunity to him..

Kundalini Thaan: This Thaan is a mysterious and novel variety where the sound vibrations are taken even deeper down than the centre of its issue, i.e., the Nabhi. After seven years of Abhyasa proved futile to achieve this Thaan, the Master had all but given it up, but his entry into the spiritual life under the Divine Maha Purusha, Swami Sivanandaji Maharaj, fired him with fresh zeal to take up the practice. And here some mysterious power helped him along and within a few months' Abhyasa day and night, Swami Nada Brahmananda attained Siddhi in the Kundalini Thaan. This was soon after he had taken holy order of Sannyas from his Gurudev Swami Sivanandaji Maharaj.

The Kundalini Thaan brings into play certain inner Pranic currents or Nadis generally not active in the majority of beings.

During this Thaan, the vibrations issue solely from the Moolaadhaara centre, at the base of the spinal column. The entire system is lulled into a state of complete quiescence. It almost seems as though the entire vocal system has taken a holiday and that no part of it above the Nabhi is involved in the production of the sound. It seems to be issuing from nowhere that we know of. A soft glow of peace and serenity suffuces the face of the Swamiji when he is engaged in producing the Kundalini Thaan.

To render the Kundalini Thaan takes some time of preliminary singing. It cannot be done off-hand at a moment's notice. It is only when the singer has his voice warmed up and the Nada gets quickened throughout the system that he attempts the Kundalini Thaan. It has got a mysterious soothing effect even upon the hearer whose mind gets slowly captivated and held by this low and humming Nada. At this time, a sense of ecstasy seems to steal over Swami Nada Brahmanandaji who, when questioned, stated that even a short practice of this Kundalini Thaan has the peculiar effect upon him of a curious, indescribable, integral satisfaction of his entire being. "I feel" said he, "as would feel a hungry man who has just feasted to his fill."

The effect of Kundalini Thaan is more psychic than physical. It achieves the cleansing of all the subtle, inner Pranic currents or in other words 'Sarva Nadi Suddhi.'

A peculiar feat: A peculiar exercise painstakingly perfected through much arduous practice demonstrates to us Swami Nada Brahmanandaji's amazing control over Nada-Sakti. It is an altogether unique feat where he sends down the vibrations of vocal Nada into remote parts of the body at will. Thus when he directs the rapid vibratory impulse of a Thaan he is executing, along the arm, it is found that the impulse travels from the centre of the sound location right along the limb to its extremity where it sets the tendons into rapid motion in perfect rhythm with the Thaan in question. At such a time the tendons at the back of his clenched fist and over the knuckles can be distinctly seen in rhythmic motion. Even as many as four pairs of muscular hands of strong young men grasping Nada Brahmanandaji's hand tightly from shoulder upto his wrist have failed to nullify the force of this Pranic impulse thus sent under the impelling power of a rapid Thaan. This phenomenon has baffled even clever medical men who, with the intention of close observation, have themselves personally joined in grasping Nada Brahmanandaji's arm during this Thaan demonstration.

Before concluding, however, one observation has to be made in respect of these Thaans mentioned above. Most of these Thaans comprise purely a Sadhana Vidya. They are usually not made in the course of public musical performances. Rather, they are primarily practised by the votary of Sangeeta Sastra as an important part of training. They are aimed at the achievement of breath control and perfection in voice culture. Their Abhyasa is in the nature of personal practice involving strenuous and intricate exercise. It is like the gymnasium work-out of a master pugilist or acrobat who aims ultimately at demonstrating *the total resultant perfection* of control, balance and action in his or her special act and feature. Thus, it will be seen that they are purely a subjective matter to the musician and their practice an integral part of his inner development upon the hard up-hill path towards perfection. It will therefore, be a mistake to seek for melody in most of these Thaans. Nevertheless, some of them do have definite musical value simultaneous with their role in the realm of breath control and voice cultivation.

Now, so far we have considered the purely technical and the therapeutical aspects of the Thaan. We shall here try to see the musical aspect of the same. In what relation the practice of Thaan stands to the culture of real music and the role it plays in imparting to the artist the gift of the voice beautiful with its thrilling richness of tone and timbre will be now seen. We may say that on the musical side the Thaan comprises a matchless foundation for the achievement of sweetness of tone, excellence in melody and superb music.

Three things combine to bestow the stamp of true greatness on a musician; his success is proportionate to the degree to which he masters these three factors. These three are firstly, the pitch with its threefold gradations of the Tara Sthayi (octave), Madhya Sthayi and the Mandara Sthayi. Secondly, the volume of voice, mainly through the modulations of which the artist is able to express the different subtle shades of Bhav. Thirdly, the tempo. It is here that the Thaan Sadhana gives wonderful help to the musician and may be said to be an indispensable requisite to one who is really serious and earnest about progressing towards perfection in voice cultivation and control. As a Sadhana it is unequalled in its ability to enable the singer to achieve mastery over the above-mentioned three factors of pitch, volume and tempo. It is the most effective means by which the singer develops volume of his voice and acquires control over Prana or breath. It is thus found to be an ideal basis upon which to build up the superstructure of perfect and enrapturing music, such as will, thrill and move the listeners with its enthralling melody, richness, admirable mastery of technique as well as superb musical value.

The test of a true master may be said to be his ability to sing well in all the three pitches, the Tara Stayi, the Madhya Stayi and Mandara Stayi as well. This he must be able to do with utmost ease, grace and perfection. He must be able to switch on from one pitch to the other with rapidity as well as unerring accuracy. There should be no blemish in his quick passage from one pitch to the other and also in his rendering of the Sahitya in each particular pitch held at the time. The difficult practice of Thaan Sadhana is of inestimable help to the musician in acquiring this rare finish. The Thaan, when thus rightly understood and intelligently and earnestly practised is the greatest friend and helper to the wise singer in his attempt to scale the high peaks of perfection in music.